Becoming The Co
'*The True, False & Fu*king Plain Stupid*'

*All the tools you need to become a great coach or professional in your field, along with all my experience, major fu*k ups and successes along the way! A Biography of my life and career.*

# Introduction

If this is the first time you've come across me, let me introduce myself. My name is Leon, I've been a Personal Trainer within the fitness industry and more recently the social media industry for a collective 12 years now. I'm most popularly known nowadays as one half of TheLeanMachines fitness duo of which the other half is my best friend and business partner John.

So why are you writing this book alone I hear you ask?

I decided to write this purely riding a wave of motivation following a long period of self reflection during the global pandemic COVID-19. Yep we all remember that bastard right, you get to read this, month's or maybe even years after it's passed but i'm still sat here in my pants writing on day one, not able to go in a shop without getting in formation, donning a mask and abiding by the invisible 2m social distance rule, crazy world. But why? I wanted and needed something to commit to that would challenge me and being dyslexic I find writing tasks a huge challenge so that's a big fat tick right there. Also I've always associated the idea of writing a book to be this huge grandiose thing which comes to you via a cheque, a deadline, a few PHD's or a huge storytelling ability which I do not possess, when i actually stripped it down to what it really is I realised it's just putting words on digital paper, and anyone can do that.

I realised what I possess is 'a particular set of skills' haha love a bit of Taken, and a lot of experience within my field. Memories, huge fuck up stories, learnings and techniques that I've developed over the years by myself and with the help of my peers, that if there were such insight shared with me as a new PT and young man stepping in the door all those years ago I think I would've saved myself a lot of embarrassment and potential court cases along the way.

You see, in the world of fitness we are all sold this idea that if we just love the gym and look decent all year round we will do well.To a certain degree that certainly helps, especially nowadays with social media. But the undeniable fact that comes round time and time again is, that 'people invest in people.'

I pride myself on being a Personal Trainer who is a human first, I will never lie to my clients about my own relationship with food and training, good or bad to make myself look perfect or at least better than them. You can become a beacon in many ways. Unfortunately I see time and time again, the method used and taught to 'instruct' is by highlighting a person's weaknesses then simply focussing on fixing them without ever exploring the reasons as to why they came about in the first place.

This (in my opinion) comes from a constant need to give results in PT. We as coaches are measured by the results our clients get and rightly so, but the results our clients get should not be measured in a 4-12 week time scale or in fact our time with them alone. Has that person continued for the next year without your help or did they just get another PT? Have they got even more from their training since learning from you? Do they still use the skills years on? Also the transformation if you want to call it that, is not always a physical or aesthetic one.

To become a great coach you need to have the confidence and self belief to be honest and frank with people, give them the time they need in order to progress and understand them beyond a surface level.... I don't mean go banging all your clients either, that never ends well! But

honestly the qualification isn't enough to succeed in this industry, you need a personality, a ton of enthusiasm and a very decent marketing strategy, of which I will share in this book. Most important of all though, you have to really want to do it. No matter how much you love training yourself if you don't get that same feeling from helping others, or even close. Don't become a coach!

WARNING - Before you read on, I'd like to warn you that I may throw the odd F bomb in here and there but it's not to appear hard or to be a lad it's just, well sometimes a solid fuck or shit really just hits the spot! I hope you won't take offence, I'm just a very passionate guy.

# CHAPTERS

# The Back Story

With this book mainly being focussed around my career as a PT and effectively a 'coaching book' I saw little value in writing about my upbringing, nor do I really like to talk about it much as I believe far too many people use their youth as an excuse or bargaining chip later in life. A bit like a poor me' attitude at times. But having listened to a good ten books this year I now realise the importance of our youth, upbringing and lifestyle not only to build a better picture for the reader but more importantly I am in part the result of all of those early years as well. When it comes to a persons current position in life good or bad, it's really easy for us to see it literally and measure our current position against it. I see multi millionaires on the daily talking about their success in business, but the decent ones also talk about their failures and their past. There seems to be a huge correlation between successful people and having not always had money in their life. I'm by no means a millionaire haha well depends on how you measure wealth, which we will get to but I don't have to steal mars bars anymore to be able to eat them..

I was born May 30th 1987 and for the first 4 years of my life I was brought up in a small cottage in a place called Eccles, living with my older sister, mum and dad. I don't remember a whole lot about living there apart from one day deciding it would be a great idea to throw tree branches at passing cars... It wasn't!
And on another day believing that calpol was not in fact medicine but a strawberry shake so I necked a whole bottle and was swiftly rushed to hospital for my efforts! LAD.
Any subsequent memories were after my mum and dad were divorced.

No matter how old you are, you understand completely the second your parents split up, without even being told, it's really strange but me and my sister just knew.

Mum couldn't afford to keep the cottage so we moved to a small town called Attleborough and for some unknown reason, out of alll the houses mum could have chosen, she chose the one connected to the side of Dodds Road Stores. Like so connected that we could sit in the living room and hear the fridges in the store through the walls. Yes, it was extremely convenient having a shop right next door but at the same time there was a constant flow of people and headlights at night until the shop closed, then from 5AM deliveries and early customers dictating your sleeping routine.

I remember this house for two reasons, one and most obviously it was the first place we lived as a trio -   me, mum and Minnie, my older sister. Two, and more uncomfortably, this was the first place I discovered I was now terrified of my dad. He still wanted to be active in our lives and would come round fortnightly to take us out for food or to get some new clothes etc but I remember a particular day I just didn't wanna go. I cried, told mum I wasn't going but dad made me, and by made me I remember him practically having to drag me to the car kicking and screaming. This may sound brutal but I think in all honesty he was just hoping I would be ok once we got on the road to Sports Mania, and he wanted to give mum a break. Except I wasn't ok.

From a young age I had a strong mind and liked to be in control of making my own decisions and for the first time in my life I felt totally helpless and out of control. The power of 'no' completely disappeared. It's funny we get brought up being told 'no means no' until the second you disagree and it suddenly doesn't matter anymore. And when I say I liked to have my own mind and be in control, I remember a particular day I wanted to test this during a shopping trip with mum. She said we could have one thing, whatever we wanted but only one thing!

We were in a cheap 99p store so the options were endless, I decided to test mum or so I thought, and picked up a foot long metal crowbar and said '*I want this!*' Thinking I was going to get resisted massively. I readied myself for a fight and mum simply replied '*ok*'. Bollocks. I'd both won and lost. I kinda wanted it, but I kinda also just wanted to stand my ground a little. Either way that crowbar was epic and came with me everywhere over the next two years.

Anyway, When I look back now I believe this was only such a 'big deal' moment because at this time I was still grieving the break up of my parents and still had no true explanation, so I did what any other totally rational and normal kid would do in my shoes, I blamed the one who left and that was dad, so it was his fault!

After that situation dad still came every week but I never went along, and this just caused him and my sister to become closer and closer, encouraging me to go even less and the dad fear continued to grow!

After about a year of being at Dodds Road, my mum needed to make some extra money so would take part in this program called Foreign Exchange, whereby kids from France who want to come explore a part of the UK can come live with a British family to learn about their way of life and in return mum gets paid for putting them up for a couple weeks. Well in a word, it was fucking awkward! Can you imagine sharing your house with a complete stranger who does not speak , nor understand a word of english and they follow you around everywhere making notes. Fuck me it done my head in so much that I would spend as much time as possible locked away in my bedroom to avoid talking.

I remember a particularly helpful guy who came to stay with us one
year who spoke a little english and seemed really nice. I had an old rust
ridden mountain bike at the time and was pretty into Teenage Mutant
Ninja Turtles so thought 'why not respray my bike green' Got hold of
some spray paint and on the day I decided to get it done mum asked me
to walk into town with her to get some shopping as she needed help with
the bags. This French guy asked if he could help with any chores so
mum offered up the job of spraying my bike for me, what
a legend I thought. I told him the areas to spray and areas to cover up
etc '*basically spray the frame mate!*'
We came back two hours later to find my bike green, like totally green
along with the white wall behind it. He'd sprayed the frame yes, but also
the wheels, spokes, tires, seat, handlebars and handles and every cable
on it.. GREEN! He was the last exchange student we had for a while!

When I was about 8 we moved to the other side of town and into our first
council house, it was a brand new build which I thought was absolutely
off the damn chain! Until the neighbour so much as thought about letting
a fart out, jeez those walls were thin! I met one of my life long friends on
that estate who I still speak to today. Woody! What a fucking legend that
boy is. 5 foot nothing, more ginger hair than I've ever seen but a great
human being, a survivor I call him. That boy and his younger brother
have been through some shit I tell ya, he's cheated death a few times
since we've been friends. Not long after I met him his mum died of can-
cer and naturally it hit them both hard. We became closer and naughtier
it has to be said. We spent our days breaking into the building site near
where we lived and snooping around, then crossing the fields near my
house to the A11,

the main dual carriageway between London and Norwich.

We upgraded that day, from me throwing old branches at cars on a back road to throwing stones at cars travelling 70mph down a motorway, hilarious! We thought cars were like tanks and would just deflect our stones like flies but making a far cooler noise! Until a police car comes past seeing 2 ginger lads and a scruffy kid pissing themselves whilst winding up a right arm to launch a stone at this stickered up car.

I've never run so fast in my life as I did that day!

We were caught, bollocked and grounded, which had little weight in either of our households so we were back in the building site by lunchtime! This was the first place I felt at home as a youngster after mum and dad split. I had friends, local friends, I knew my area well and fitted in at school, it was pretty sweet by all accounts.

Then we moved again....
Only this time it was 20 miles up the A11 to Norwich City to a place called Costessey! I was 2 weeks into year 5 at school, so 9/10 years old. Most kids were in their groups or clicks by then and the pace of life felt totally different as well. If you were an academic kid you were like a genius amongst men. If you were a naughty kid in the city,(I thought I was simply going to slot into that group - I was wrong) you were also a bully by default, ran the playgrounds, and nicked sweets from the local stores as standard. You could buy your popularity in sherbet straws.

Absolute game changer going from a small town to a city at any age, let alone just before you start gearing up for high school, finding your first few hairs on ya balls and now suddenly having to get a bus to school in a place you don't know, I was out of my depth to say the least.

In that first term of year 5 or what was left of it, was where I practically lost my ability to talk and started using my physical ability to fit in instead. I was quickly set upon by the school bullies for wearing cheap charity shop clothes and for not being from around there, reason enough I guess. After being pulled around the playground a few times by my hair, which was long and slicked back at the time (didn't do myself any favours really), they got bored of not getting much back so luckily for me, it just stopped. My luck continued as I became very good at throwing a cricket ball and broke every record the school ever held. I won local sports events which in turn came with a huge elevation in social status! It was the prequel to throwing a javelin that for obvious reasons we couldn't go near until we were at high school.

Junior school went pretty well and I gained some decent friends. Then two things happened, one...yes we moved again, to a place called Cloverhill in Bowthorpe. I didn't think anything of it but according to the kids it was a very rough part of our local area, great. And two, we were about to go on to a new school, High School where we would now be the youngest in the school.

Apologies, I kind of glazed over the reason we moved to Bowthorpe..

Our time living in Costessey was different to say the least and what went down during that time taught me a lot about the world and I matured as a result. It also switched on an area of my being called empathy that I didn't truly appreciate until I was older and working with people.

Excited to be in the city, my mum went all out and wanted to get us Sky tv (which she couldn't really afford) ! That meant someone had to come round, hang a dish and set up the cables etc. This guy was Mark, my beautiful younger sister's father... Well that gives away the part where he first becomes my mum's boyfriend doesn't it. They dated for a while, he had a bit of an unhealthy love for smoking weed and low and behold that soon turned into my mum smoking as well. Everything seemed quite normal for a while, I genuinely thought he was pretty cool, and he made my mum happy so I had no issue. Then things got weird, like really weird. I'm not sure if it was the weed that triggered it or he was just an unwell guy, but he started becoming aggressive and sporadic with mum, us and just in general. I'd often walk into a room thinking he was on the phone but he was legit having a full blown conversation with himself, even escalating and getting angry with the invisible response. Things got worse to the point where he fitted a lock on my bedroom door and would randomly tell me and my sister to get in our room and lock us in for periods of time, then get into a screaming match with my mum before coming back calm as you like and letting us out again.

One night I remember he flipped and locked us in, my bedroom looked over the back garden which backed straight onto an open field. We heard the back door go so I looked out my window to see him practically dragging my mum into the field. WTF! Everything went quiet for a while, we heard the odd raised voice here and there over the next half hour until they came walking back and let us out. But only for him to shuffle us straight into the back of his work van where he laid down a single mattress for us to be comfortable, and then we drove. (This was called the 'sooty van' when things were good). He drove the exact same loop around the city turn for turn, two maybe three times until he felt safe' apparently before returning home. I won't divulge more of that time because it's not all my story to tell but let's just say it was a mess and we all learnt a lot, and fuck me the love and respect I have for my mum was solidified at that time.

He was a paranoid schizophrenic who was convinced my mum worked for the secret service and was spying on him. The episode where he dragged her into the field, he could see tanks and soldiers in the fields hiding and coming for him… dark shit!

When I talk about empathy, once I'd grown up and learnt a little more about the world and myself within it, I looked back and found myself feeling sorry for him. That bloke dragged our family through the dirt and then left mum to pick up the pieces and run and hide to a new house. But I still felt sorry, maybe it's because had that not have happened I wouldn't have my younger sister here today so i'm thankful, who knows.

Moving to Bowthorpe didn't have too much effect on the school situation, to be honest it probably helped as I was then walking/ cycling distance from school instead of busing it in! Bowthorpe was the type of place whereby having a mum like mine and an older sister like mine really helped, they both had big mouths, mum loved to gossip and my sister was an absolute badass! Mum knew everything that was going on around ours and the two streets either side of us, she bloody knew everyone and had a skill, product or general gossip attached to each of them. Number 26 could get hold of any wholesale item you wanted, number 14 always had knock off trainers and secondhand kit and number 36 had to be a lady of the night or a drug dealer as people were always coming and going. At this time there was a gang forming in Bowthorpe that called themselves the ATL crew, my sister knew a few of the guys but certain areas suddenly became areas you didn't go. Being a young gang trying to make a name for themselves they were pretty reckless and would often go out looking to beat people up for no apparent reason or robbing etc so I steered clear, like very clear.

I remember a time I was cycling towards the shops via a cut through and saw 3 of them sitting on the wall about 30m up from me and it was a swift stop, turn around and ride the other way. I was called and shouted from the second they saw me but I knew damnn well my bike was going and a black eye was coming if I carried on, choose your battles! It was a good idea that i never went near them at that point because not even a year later one of the guys walked up to me at a local park and pulled a knife and told me to give him my BMX (my pride and joy), I refused which could've been a really bad idea but luckily as i cast my gaze up from the knife to his faced I recognised him. He had been and knocked round for my sister before, I swiftly pulled the 'you know my sister card' and he swiftly let go of my neck when i told him her name. Close call.

At that age physically I was capable but i couldn't fight my way out of a wet paper bag, hilarious considering my dad was an ex top British super middleweight boxer and often featured on Sky Sports in the late 80's and early 90's. But we will talk about why I got into boxing after I tell you about high school.

I rolled up to my first week thinking I was a bit of a lad in all honesty. I had friends, one of which a guy called Max who became a great friend of mine, lived a couple doors down and the first lad I idealised as a young man. You know the one, tall, handsome and had the right hair cut at the right time 'stud'. We're still friends to this day and he has still supplied the funniest thing I've ever witnessed in my whole life involving him a moped and a garden fence, but I'll save that story for another day. None of the other years were there to begin with. They set it up this way so for a few days the newbies could get used to the school and find their way around. Also my sister was already at the school and had a solid place in the naughty crew or (cool kids) crew. That ended up not being ideal as she also hated school and had some major run-ins with certain teachers that saw my last name and presumed me to be very much the same, until proven otherwise.

*The Back Story*

She was expelled not long after my arrival so her being there was no help, haha I still remember the first week with all the kids there, it was intense, I felt like a midget and man were the corridors busy.

I also had a bit of a cocky attitude by this age, mouthy some would call it. You learn fast in a public high school - be mouthy and fight or be mouthy and fast, so you can run away. Running worked the first couple times I decided to kick the cool year 11 lads shins as I walked past, or tried to trip them up 'for bants'. Then I tripped the wrong lad, Luke. He was a cool kid but also a bit of a fucking unit as well and loved a fight. He grabbed me by my backpack before I had a chance to run, swung me round like a rag doll then proceeded to do the same while holding my ever growing hair. I got a good pasting that day from him and his mates, well deserved to be honest! So well deserved in fact, that I actually hunted both him and another lad from the group down before i'd left school and thanked them for the kick-in, as had it not happened, then it probably would've come worse down the line. I suddenly knew my place, it's true in every school or social group, there is a pecking order and the sooner you find your place the better it will be!

After this the early years of high school were pretty much as expected, I excelled in sport - running and football specifically and excelled with the ladies also. We were all part of this big social group of around 20, practically a 50/50 split of boys and girls. I think we all must've dated each other at some point, it was so incestuous it was hilarious. But honestly, some of my best younger years were spent with members of that group. First proper snogs, hand jobs disguised as red torture games and truth or dares consisting of only dares because we all wanted to be dared to go and do 60 seconds of touchy feely with the boy or girl we fancied round the corner.

I'm telling ya there is nothing stranger than a bunch of horny teenagers playing games! I sit here with a cheeky smile at just the thought of what we were all up to, haha brilliant!

It was at the age of 12/13 where I started to separate my home Leon from my school Leon, a shit time to be completely honest and I do feel a little ashamed that I allowed social norms and popularity to screw my view on what was important in life, this won't be the last time as you will realise reading on. We lived in a council estate and our house was a bit of a mess as standard really, my mum was skint working nights and all her very little money she did in fact have, went on buying us the stuff we thought we needed to fit in but she couldn't afford! The start of each school year came with a mountain of stress for her knowing damnn well we needed' Kickers or Pods on our feet and Fila as bare minimum as a backpack to avoid getting shit from the other kids. That would come in anyway it needed to, borrowing from high interest doorstep loan sharks or working a second job, she made it happen. Also my mum is one of the worlds best charity shoppers, i'm telling you now she can find a  bargain anywhere. She used to call it 'charity bashing' and would plan days and weekends of it going out with friends with a tenner in her pocket and coming back with a good £50 quids worth of stuff! I still remember my first pair of running spikes I so desperately needed to take my running more seriously coming in the form of a pair of charity shop brought Pumas that were at least one size too big for me. In order for them not to slip off I had to wear two thick pairs of socks and tie the laces so tight i could hardly feel my feet, but they worked! Bargain! This started a trend that JC ripped me for for years of 'double socking.'

I became embarrassed by our situation because I was hanging around with the perfect family kids. The yearly Disney world trip kids for the most part and the kids whose family just had money, well enough to pay for the stuff we all wanted without having to borrow it anyway. So I

proceeded to do a few things in order to 'keep up with the Joneses' as such. I would only ever show my head at the door when friends came to knock. I would literally have an indent of the front door on the right side of my face it was pressed so hard against me, embarrassed to let

anyone see inside where the walls were half painted. I moaned like hell to mum until she moaned to the council to change our front door,

because it was unsafe after nearly being kicked in by her ex. I knew that if we had a new door we could paint it, clear up the front walk way and give it a shred of curb appeal.

Then I decided to stop telling people where I lived, even gave some of my friends the wrong address so they'd never be able to come knock for me. This was helped even more so when a council house came up in the next close and mum took it, only 40 metres from our old place but far enough that all my mates who knew my old address now didn't know my new one, apart from Max. I'm sure to this day if you asked my mum, she

couldn't tell you a single person who knocked for me on that door from the age of 13-17 apart from Max. Sorry mum there was a reason for that.

I remember this time as being the first big junction in my life for a few reasons. A definable point whereby I started to fall inside myself and clam up when away from my friends. I see this in teens more and more these days. I hit that point and it was because of the invisible pressure being turned up in my head that never really existed.

An age where we are judged on labels, brands, and physical skills, so much so we will do almost anything possible to earn points and status. I believe that many youngsters walk away from their true identity in order to fit in, which causes major internal conflict and separation later in life. That's a whole other subject, but that's just my opinion.

This was also when the bed wetting started getting worse, yep you heard me right. It wasn't actually until writing this book and really looking over my whole life with a small telescope did I really start to understand the real reasons behind some of my behaviours as a young teen I used to simply label 'hormones'. I'd wet the bed and had the odd accident as I was growing up but it got worse around high school and I also started another strange activity around the same time. If i'd ever had a bad day, argument or fall out with anyone that required an emotive response other than a full on fight, I would creep up into our partly converted loft. Partly' meaning there were giant sheets of ply just laid across the beams haha and I would light a candle and gently pour it over my hands, let it dry then peel it off. I looked at it as a fun game and it was very satisfying just peeling it off as well I must say. But the more I looked back the more I started to piece together the times it would happen and realised it was actually more a form of self harm. I was a kid that couldn't deal with big emotions, I'd never been taught to, we were a family that shut up and got on with it, so I found new coping mechanisms. The wax was hot enough to feel something but not so hot that it would leave physical scars, I was a calculated self harmer which is even more fucked up when I think about it.

The bed wetting was more of a release I think. A whole day of trying so hard to be someone else requires a lot of effort and stress, that when I could finally relax… my bladder would as well! This didn't help in some social aspects, sleepovers were a no go for me. Well even more so as the first one I went to I pissed the bed and actually had to hide the sheet and my shame so no one would know. Never went to another after that.

Aged 12 I started a Sunday paper round, anyone who had one of those knows damnn well they were the heaviest day of the week with the broad sheets and weekly television schedules in as well as the usual gossip shit. It was such a heavy round I had to do it in two halves to begin with as I couldn't get all the papers in one, all that for £3 a week! But it was structure and a way of earning my own money. I then also began working weekends and school holidays for my dad. I stupidly thought this was all about reestablishing our bond and relationship, but it was about work and the values I gained from the process.

Working with my dad taught me at a very young age the true value of money or not money but what if offers. To start with I didn't work for payment I worked towards something I wanted. Dad would ask '*what do you want right now*' '*err I want this BMX, Haro backtrail x3*' to be exact. He'd check the price and then say '*ok in ten days work we'll go and get you it!*' I'd do my ten days and low and behold on day 11 he took me there to pick it up, no money exchanged hands, I wish life was able to continue that way for longer. My dad has taught me many things throughout my life but that job was the start of many things. Money, strength, commitment and hard working attitude.

I think it's about time we talk about skip jumping don't you….

At the age of 13 I was earning a couple quid every now and then with dad on top of the things' I wanted to work for which felt great but when I did get cash I was still far too young to really appreciate it enough to hold on to it, so I was still always skint. Mum heard through the grapevine that Roys near us always threw food in the skips out back as soon as it hit one day beyond its shelf date. Most food lasts far longer than that, apart from fish and poultry, we always avoided that stuff just in case.

So mum did her research and found out what days and what foods were being skipped and once they'd closed up i'd don a backpack, jump over the wall and fill it full of stuff. Bread, donuts, anything I could cram in. Donuts tended to be a bit hard but 10 seconds in the microwave, i'm telling ya BANGIN!! This became a weekly occurrence, resulting in separating my home life from school life even more so. I mean, can you imagine what would happen if i told my mates at school that I was doing that!! But I wanted to make mum smile and help out a bit so that's all that mattered.

I did this at Roys and a Mr Kipling factory on the industrial estate about a kilometre run from mine for about a year. Kipling's had to throw away anything that was deformed or slightly less aesthetic so I was constantly balls deep in French Fancies for a good year.... Before they caught on! I was going later and later to both as security started turning up knowing what we and others were starting to do. When I started setting my alarm for 4/5am I was turning up at the same time as the early shift workers, the gig was up and skip jumping was no more! Fucking great times though and a great rush running and diving head first into a skip not knowing if you're about to be ripped out by the scruff of you neck, bitten by a rat or finding a 24 tray of ring donuts!

I then hit my angry stage 'peak testosterone' with nowhere to direct it! I started to struggle with the two way life I was living, hiding things from my friends, hating our living situation so much that I found myself almost blaming mum when she was only doing her best, which came with another layer of guilt. So I started getting in fights more often. I remember a biblical scrap I had with a good friend Chris after taking the piss out of him for being tall for a good hour, I knew he'd snap eventually and boy did he! He chased me down and we embarked on this pathetic attempt at a fight, strangling each other, pulling each other's hair and swinging wildly.

We only made contact with a fist or two and were too exhausted to continue any longer.

Thankfully at this point we were separated by friends, who had of course let it play out for a while for their pleasure! As I shuffled home convinced i'd smashed him up, getting my title winning story ready for the following day to spread round the playground I remember feeling this rush, a very addictive buzz! Was it the fight, my supposed win or just the release? All I knew is that it felt good, so I continued trying to get in fights for myself and even others where I could. I became extremely mouthy and would start disrupting my lessons just because I wanted to be a twat.

Despite this, I gained enough respect across the board that I became a prefect in year 11. Our school had this system, (mainly because it was a school in special measures and the young kids got bullied hard!!) that your form was of staggered ages, 4 or 5 kids from each year group, with one male and one female in year 11 that were given the title and purple polo shirt to go with it, of prefect. This was a way of giving the younger kids someone to turn to who was not a teacher if they were bullied or wanted some advice, a great system often abused by popular kids. I still wanted to fight and had my bad ass punch bag hung up at home too, so at this point I thought I was the tits.

When a young year 7 lad came to me crying one day because a boy in my year had tripped him up in the corridor for seemingly no reason at all, I couldn't wait to get my Ali attitude out. I told the kid to take me to him and point him out, off we marched round the school like rabid dogs hunting for blood. My heart was racing, lips and mouth dry, I couldn't wait to hit this kid. We found him tucked up in a maths class hiding as he had been told I was looking for him, news travels fast in high school.

At this point a voice in my head said 'look just call him a dick, threaten him a bit and ' WHACK! Yep I just whacked him, turned on my heels and walked back out again like an absolute boss convinced what i'd done was the right thing. To this day I will be honest and say he deserved the slap he got for sure but unfortunately my reasonings for doing it were only 50% to protect or avenge the young year 7. The other 50% were my own, I wanted it, I wanted to hurt him!

It ended up with me spending a week in isolation - which  means you go to school as you usually would, but your whole time is spent in a room with one teacher and the other little shits of the school, in complete silence all day!

Got away quite lightly considering the school had a zero tolerance for bullying. I wonder if this was down to the fact that my head teacher was a pedophile who had a soft spot for my then partner. He would constantly have her in his office, questioning what we "got up to together". Which was enough reason to let me stay and keep me happy I guess.

I am being 100% straight up here, It came out a couple years after I left school, the teacher in question got one of the year 9 students pregnant, which blew his cover. There was then a stream of young girls that came forward sharing stories about how he'd randomly started pulling them out of classes, take them to his office and ask intimate questions about them. Fuck I wish my X told me about it at the time, I was peak Ali wannabe, i'd have had him!

I had to keep my nose clean from there on out if I wanted to leave with GCSE's so I got my head down, hit the bag at home and trained a lot of my anger and frustrations out.

When I left school i'd been offered a place in sixth form to study business and human biology with the hopes at that point to become a PE teacher after admiring the 3 or 4 i'd gotten to know over the years in my time. Or a paramedic. I went for 3 days before I sacked it off and went full time working for my dad. Why? I was earning £40 a day at 16 years old and all I had to pay for was the £4 full tank of fuel for my moped! I think many young angry idiots with an identity issue and a huge lack in confidence would've done the same in my situation!

After getting in a couple of fights, and generally just being angry, dad took me to the boxing club i'd end up fighting through, The Lads Club. Great gym, great people and some real life lessons and respect earnt and found in there. It's an extremely humbling experience the first time you step in a ring to face off with someone you were having a lovely conversation with 5 minutes prior. Who had no reason to fight you but would willingly now spark you out if you drop your guard for a second. A planned fight in a ring is 1000% harder and more respect worthy than a pissed up brawl on the street because you have to control your emotions, ow and do the whole thing totally sober as well.

To begin with, boxing sent me in the wrong direction and I got in more fights outside of training and thought I was the tits. That changed one night I ended up becoming protector for another young kid who was bullied in a town I grew up in. All us older boys saddled up to find the twat who was our age, my role was always going to be the muscle, stand there and look hard while his brother whacked him. If any of his mates got involved that's when i'd step in… What happened?! Around ten seconds into another lad giving him the hairdryer treatment i'd stepped in and whacked him two times before he'd even hit the deck… out cold!

We walked, then we ran, I was hustled into a car and driven out of town fast. I can genuinely say the way that lad fell I thought i'd killed him, one of the most sobering moments of my life in fact. I was now terrified, frantically contacting everyone who was around to find out if an ambulance came, is he awake? has he called the cops if he is? Finally my mate sully got a text saying he was just knocked out and came round but went straight home to tell his older brother who said, this is great by the way 'Why the fuck are you picking fights with him for?!" Lol. The very next day I woke up and had only one thing on my mind, I had to apologise, for no other reason than the horrific guilt of what could've been had sunk well and truly in and I couldn't bare it. I found the lad sporting one hell of a shiner and apologised, he also accepted some of the blame himself because he could see that he was being a dick for no reason. It was quite a special moment for me as I walked away from that situation feeling just as hyped as if I had been fighting, the only difference was a sense of pride and manliness that also came with it. It felt good to lay myself bare, admit that I was in the wrong and not get torn down for it. Two young men met with hate and pain and left with respect through using one thing, words.

After that night I left most of my fighting in the ring and really enjoyed it for the structure and discipline. I trained 6 days a week 3 at the club and 3 with dad. We'd run between 4 and 6 miles followed by 3 rounds of 50 sit ups, 50 push ups and 50 Russian twists, all performed next to each other with our feet tucked under my nans bed where we were living at that point.

It wasn't long before I became what they call 'a carded boy' which meant I would now be taking fights from other clubs or competitions outside the club, basically I was taking it seriously.

I won my first two fight pretty convincingly, happy days! Then there was a long spell without a fight but I really didn't care because at around the same time 3 lads walked in the club who scared the absolute shit outa me, the real deal. The Walsh brother, if you know boxing you will have heard of them, proper badass fighters all 3 of them. Michael was the lighter of the 3, boxing in the mid 50kg classes if I remember correctly and he'd come in that club early (like me) pick up his rope and would just go like he was on a mission. I'd try my best to keep up with him and held my own until they put us in the ring together. Fuck me he hit me from angles physics couldn't understand! I knew he was gonna go far, and he did! Well they all did in fact!

I left boxing after an on off relationship with it spanning over 3-4 years. A mixture of not really feeling the WOW after a win or FUCK YEAH hunger when a fight came in like I knew I really should. And booze and women started!

The above were not the real reason/s I left boxing, it's just what I told myself for years. The real reason was simple, I never really wanted to do it in the first place, well not beyond the conditioning and learning how to look after myself if I needed to. I knew I was different to the rest of the boys, and my dad. They all wanted to fight, couldn't wait to get in there and just fuck their opponent up, they almost needed that aggression in their life like a drug, i'd lost that after that' night in town. I was just a classic young lad with daddy issues, yes guys have them too. I wanted to impress my old man in any way I could once I started working with him. I think I almost wore this cloak of guilt for all the years I refused to go anywhere with him after him and my mum split, and i'd do anything to get his trust, respect and love back, even though it had never gone.

There's one more part of my upbringing I want to talk about before we get into the Real Shit. You will hear me speaking about a time I call 'Leon On Self Destruct' There was a LOT of things going on around this time, I don't think there's enough pages for me to really' go into them all, so I have focussed my time on what I call key moments.

This final key moment from my youth has taught me more about the fragility of life and consequences of actions or inactions more than any single other time in my life. So after fucking up my training with boxing by going out and getting absolutely smashed with my mates every weekend, a key one of which being a good friend Jamie. Man we had some times! We were some of the eldest in our group of boys so turned 18 first, and we had a few quid in our pockets! We had a weekly routine that lasted, I kid you not 8 months. Every single Friday and Saturday night i'd pick him up, we'd drive to Sainsbury's near my mums in Bowthorpe for vodka and cheap ass redbull, pick up a Mc Donalds and head to hers to drink a whole bottle each whilst playing James Bond Golden Eye on the n64. We'd then get in a cab around 7.30 and go to the exact same drinking spots and stand in the exact same place every night. Always finishing in Mercy hammered on one of the stages. We'd even throw in the odd Thursday if the work load was looking a little light the next day, you see he was a chippy (carpenter) and I was a roof tiler and we'd often bump into each other on site. There is one part I kinda missed out though…

So every now and then he would have to work Saturdays and would ask me to go grab him a hundred quid out of his savings account. 'No worries', i'd take his book, withdraw the cash at the till and simply sign his name, no biggy! Until the day I went in to get the cash and unknowingly to me, his auntie not only worked there, she served me! Yep! Told me if I didn't get Jamie on the phone in 5 minutes the cops were going to be called, thankfully it all got straightened out and we lived to laugh about the story.

This key moment happened on a night like many other with our group of lads. The phones would be pretty quiet until about lunch time then 'what's the plan' would start getting dropped. Followed by the banter of whose going to out drink who, lad stuff ya know! My life long friend woody was already out with another friend of ours Rob. We didn't hang out with him all the time he was one of the skater crew who was actually a cool as fuck lad who loved to get pissed as well as stoned. Those two were close and were out in the city celebrating Rob turning 18 and his first BIG night! They were smashed by the time we all met them, so me and the lads started playing catch up. Being gym lads by this point we were pretty solid lightweights as well so it's fair to say a couple of us sent it a little hard. My mate B got turned away from Mercy and I was pretty smashed too so said fuck it home time let's go! Woody and Rob carried on until some crazy time in the morning, I even think some cctv cameras in a car park caught them at like 3am or something.

I woke up the next day hanging out of my ring like any other weekend, then did the usual text round to laugh about the states we were in from the night before, then got on with my day…. Doing as little as possible. Around lunchtime it started. The boys started texting asking if we'd heard from Rob, then his girlfriend and other skate lads were asking and calling woody about him saying they'd not heard from him, he never came home. I then received a call that changed my life, by far the worst hangover i've ever had. A body of a young lad had been found in the river that runs through the city behind a few of the night clubs. His best mate was asking me frantically 'what was he wearing?' and when i last saw him that night. I told him the truth we were all fucked up and I went home early with B.

I put the phone down and my trainers on in the same action, I needed air! My phone was going insane at this point, every one of us who was out and saw him that night felt responsible in some way. The news broke a couple days later naming Rob as the 18 year old who drowned. It was said that he had so much alcohol in his system he could've actually died of alcohol poisoning which caused a secondary ripple effect as only weeks before 24 hour drink licensing rules had been announced, the shit hit the fan. It turned out that woody was the last person standing with Rob which to this day I hate for him as I know he carries a lot of guilt still wrongly. They made their way to some black cabs that were always about, woody put his head in the window to speak to the driver about the cost to get back to Attleborough, by the time he took his head back out Rob was gone, just like that. Woody looked for him but never found him. This moment changed life in a heartbeat. It was so fucked up what happened to Rob that night but what it taught me at a young age is unbelievable. I will 'never' take my life for granted, I truly understand the phrase 'you are never promised tomorrow' it's just unfortunate I and our friends had to learn it that way.

I'm going to leave it there with the back story, there is more and you will hear snippets throughout.

Let's get into it.

## The Real Sh!t

I will be honest, I've practically finished the first draft of the book at the point you're reading this, I started writing this chapter right at the end book and it just didn't feel right. None of what you are going to read, learn and implement means anything if you don't truly have an understanding of self and hear a few hard facts first. So I switched it on its head.

Who are you, I mean really? This is a question I often find myself asking during periods of self reflection, and... self loathing to be honest. There is no point trying to help anyone without first asking this question and getting a raw honest answer back.

Until I was in my late twenties, I believed i had all my shit in order and was well and truly on the treadmill of life. I had a great partner, the business model seemed pretty solid and I was looking into buying my second property and getting that all so important 'next' step' on the property ladder. I'd somehow managed to get this far in life without ever really asking too many questions of myself mentally. But why? The world has this quite magical rhythm whereby (in my opinion) if you go to work, work damnn hard and do mostly the right things for the right reasons in your mind, it tends to work out, to a certain degree anyway. Some naive on lookers also call it 'luck' or being lucky.

We have a culture of grow up, get a job, buy a house, get married and have kids. Then go on all inclusive family holidays to sunny Europe until they're 16 and sick of hanging with mum and dad, then mid life crisis, boom! If you are ticking that list off, I believe your head will never feel the need to pose the question of who you are and what you're really here for?

I call this the comfort zone of life (not self). Some people absolutely love living their life in this space and live a perfectly happy life there, that's just not me! If you're a driven person who wants more from yourself then write this down and put it somewhere you can remind yourself of it time and time again. The big thing i realised when I asked this question properly was that, the person I was becoming was the one everyone else wanted me to be, not who i wanted to be.

Just before we move on I want to talk about that treadmill of life and use a certain example to help open your mind up a little if you're still struggling with the idea, I call it having your head stuck in the bubble.

Here's a question for you;

*Who are houses built for?*

I was listening to a business and lifestyle coach talking about investment strategies and how to live your best life when he asked the person interviewing him this question and the answer blew my mind.
The interviewer answered much like the rest of us would, I'm sure
*'well obviously they're built for us, for humans to inhabit'.* Well on the surface yes this was correct but the real answer is, banks!

You see banks are held up by their credit system and and effectively how much money they are owed and consistently paid by you or I plus interest, like loan sharks in suits without the death threats. When banks first started offering loans to people it was to help start up companies, support farmers and help businesses to expand, but not everyone is starting businesses everyday, so they needed more income. Along came the humble 'mortgage' *'What we will do is offer people the money to buy their house, but not just their house but a bigger one.*

*One that they can't really afford right now but we will keep the*

*repayments low enough to make it manageable. But here's the kicker, in order for the payments to be low enough the mortgage has to be longer. 20-30 years long in fact.'* If I could sign up every client as a coach

knowing they were pretty much tied in for the next 30 years haha i'd lean back in my fat arm chair and drink a whiskey or two as well. Basically homes are built for banks for us to inhabit not the other way round how it so often is seen. This shook me to the core as I was looking at upgrading and buying the so called 'forever home' at the same time as writing this.

It would've involved selling both properties and still getting a huge

mortgage in order to make it happen, but it felt normal, like the next step. Now i'm sat here looking at bungalows and places on the edge of the water instead. Why put more financial pressure on myself and wife when I could be mortgage free? Because that's what we do when we are too tuned to what the world want us to became over who we want to be.

### 'Am I Being Today Who I'm Supposed To Become Tomorrow?'

The very minute I started to ask this question and honestly challenge myself and ego, my life and outlook completely changed. To this day it's the hardest thing i've ever done and at times very VERY uncomfortable, I hate being wrong! But it needed to be done as quite simply I was very unhappy with who i was trying to be in relation to who I was truly supposed to become.

People often say 'true potential is found just beyond your comfort zone' you've all seen the similar pictures of a large circle labelled 'comfort zone' then a tiny ball just outside labelled 'magic' or 'true potential'.

I would actually relabel these as the big circle 'who you try to be and how much energy it takes' Vs the small circle 'who you are supposed to be and how much energy it really takes'.

You see to me the comfort zone is not to be broken through and freed from, far from it. My goal is to expand my comfort zone as much as I possibly can in every direction to absorb and grow as much as possible, at the same time utilising both my inherent strengths and weaknesses to my power along the way. The same can not be said for your true identity and who you really are. We often hide from ourselves embarrassed or worried as to what people might think or say if we really poke our head out so we hide like naked mole rats in the soil that is our own head. Like it really matters?! But i've been there on so many levels and it's fucking exhausting and it earnt me very little respect and true connections in life.

You may have picked this book up thinking 100% that you wanted to become a PT or, a PT thinking this was it, the magic book or even a general gym goer looking for the magic answer to ignite your love for training. But after asking yourself that question properly you may well now be in a state of panic thinking' …shit is this what I really wanted or am I just doing it because it's easy or the right thing?"...safe. If I've just ruined your career or potential career, you're welcome. Because all i've actually done is help you take one step closer to yourself and what you're truly supposed to be doing with your life. It can sound brutal to some but the path of least resistance doesn't work for everyone all of the time, in my experience it tends to lead me to a soft, easy cruising like place otherwise labelled the comfort zone or cruise control.

'*Cruise control has its place in life, like on a 50mph limit on an average speed camera ridden road, perfect! But your life is a private racing track, starting with no speed limits, no traffic coming in the opposite direction and no others to race with.* You *are the only person who has full control of that track as well. Who comes on and off, how their driving impacts yours and if they can even be on the damnn track with you in the first place!*

## Why PT?

I've been asked many times why i became a PT and not for the wholesome reason you'd expect either. Nine times out of ten I'm asked in a way that people could not quite wrap their head around the fact that I would quit a pretty well paid job as a roof tiler (around £2,000 a month at it's best) to go and work the graveyard and weekend shifts as effectively a glorified receptionist for £850 per month in my first gym job, 'it just doesn't make sense mate.' Can't quite believe it, but we're arriving at the first lesson already, so pin your ears back.

The reason i always have and always will give is simple, because I now don't hear my alarm at 6am and wake up feeling pissed off and wishing it would just rain so I could go back to bed, I actually get up earlier than that most days now, or go to bed every night frantically checking the weather apps hoping it would say it was forecast to rain so I could message my boss and try talking him out of getting up. Which never worked by the way, I actually just made things worse by essentially giving him the heads up to plan wet jobs just in case... bollocks! Now however, I wake up ready to go and I'm excited most days, yes I still have shit ones where I really don't fancy it and want to lay in bed all day but fortunately I have a young daughter and a very driven wife who take care of that straight away!

I never have nor will ever say that i'm ashamed of my trade days or wish i'd never done them, not at all. I'm so proud to have that in the back pocket and god I loved my boss Bud, but I can say with 100% certainty knowing how much I don't want to go back to that world drives me forward every damn day.

Before worrying about pay packages, status or rank within the firm and social group or even benefits and perks that come with any job, the first thing you should always start by asking is 'does this make me sick nervous but so excited i could combust?'

If the answer is yes you know that it's the right direction to head in to start looking for the next

answer. I hate the saying of '*truly successful people run towards the fire not away from it*' because I don't know about you but i never see a fire and think 'ye fuck it let's go take a dip in that!' I get the point behind it but what i say to people is, '*if the idea makes you equally sick with fear and enthusiasm keep going*'.

Before I sit here sounding all preachy and woke, easy when you've done it mate ey, it wasn't like that back then. Quite honestly before i started the process to become a PT I was a bit of a mess mentally to be completely straight up. In the couple of years leading up to taking the plunge I was spending all my wages and smashing high interest rate credit cards on clothing and booze to gain social status amongst friends.

It wasn't even like the groups I hung around with gave a fuck what I wore but for me I felt I needed it, like a cloak of Burberry bling armour. I was so painfully insecure in my appearance and spent 100% of every conversation I had questioning and berating myself throughout.

Example, I could be mid conversation with someone and my internal monologue was calling myself a useless embarrassing piece of shit and telling myself to shut up because I sounded false and stupid. It sounds a pinch insane if you think of it literally, but looking back i think in all

honesty it was the start of a gift I feel i've now a positive relationship with. To be innately aware of oneself, sounds really up my own ass I know but when I look back, I was just talking shit and my head was just telling me the truth. Doing and saying anything i could, to be seen as a guy who had it all under control and essentially had the world at his feet when it simply wasn't true.

As horrible and stupid as it sounds I think I actually wanted people to think I was better than them because in some twisted way I thought it might make me think I was better too. It didn't, it just spiralled out of control to the point where I was paying off credit cards, living in my overdraft and sleeping around any time I was single just to feel something and boost the ego.

At my worst point of what I affectionately call *'Leon on self destruct mode'* I bumped into my X partner in a nightclub by sheer chance. You know the one from school, first love, first time' the lot. Very precious and dangerous people to bump into pissed out of your face in that frame of mind. A simple conversation ended up in a kiss, whiiich was interrupted by her then boyfriend and crew. I decided that I was not in the wrong and kicked RIGHT off, but upon reflection I was just as in the wrong as my X partner in this situation, it was a dick move at a dick time.

This did however lead to a 4 year re relationship (can I call it that) fuck ye I can it's my book, a re relationship where I still say to this day i'm thankful for. Because I remember still carrying on just the same as I was prior to that chance meeting and she said straight up, stop acting like a twat and we can be together, or continue alone. WOW straight up ultimatum shiz right there. This was the start of the tide of change and growth for me.

After travelling together our relationship sadly broke down but the amount of respect I have for her and those times are endless due to what i learnt about myself before, during and after. Another thing I learnt as I grew up was that just because a relationship or friendship breaks down it doesn't mean you have to hate that person in order to move forward.

If a person doesn't wrong you in life, sometimes even if they do remember to hate is very easy but extremely tiring as well. I used to block anyone out who apparently wronged me because it was easier to hate than face the idea of being civil with someone who knew me beyond a surface level, god forbid maybe even talking it out. I used to think if I let my guard down they'd just slate me, or out me in any way they could. The truth is most people just want to get on with their life and it's far easier for both parties to respect one another and their history, life goes on right.

6 months before choosing to travel, the UK went into a recession and the building industry essentially crashed over night it would seem. I remember sitting in the van one lunch break absolutely smashing in a sausage roll and stuffing prawn cocktail crisps in round the outside of it like I hadn't eaten in months whilst Buds (my old boss) phone just kept ringing. Literally it was call after call off building firms and private jobs cancelling their work. I think we must've gone from a good 4-5 months of work to the job we were on and a couple loose ends… fuuuck I thought. But at the same time the amount of faith I had in Bud I was like "well what we gonna do then mate" like he had all the bloody answers. 'whatever we have to mate. Scaffolding, gardening and odd jobs if needs be until it picks up again!' That wasn't the answer I wanted, well not that day anyway.

That was the first time I had clarity in my life and to this day i've no idea why it came whilst I was slowly choking on a sausage and prawn cocktail moosh but I just decided that day with my partner that fuck it we'll travel, get away and see the world then come back after this has all washed over. Yes of course mum helped me pay for my trip because I was still skint, good ol mum!

But in that 6 months I saved hard and also qualified as a level 2 Fitness Instructor along the way with the idea of scoping out gyms in Australia and maybe heading back over there to start my career. That was short lived as 99.9% of the trip myself and everyone I was around was fucking smashed or jumping out of planes, and I wouldn't change it for the world.

Travelling taught me a lot about myself but mostly it taught me that I could be 100% me and people would still want to be around me.
Travelling strips you bare, sometimes literally as well... Don't believe me? Listen to this;

Me and my partner at the time had arranged to hire a camper-van for two weeks of our journey down south from Brisbane to Sydney. When we turned up to the reception, everything we owned in our huge backpacks, the whole reception desk was covered in photos of naked couples and groups with only props covering their tackle. WTF is this all about we asked? 'Ow did you not read that if you get naked for a snap you get a day's rental free!' 'HOLD MY FUCKING BEER!' We went and got our kit off, took a photo and saved an extra 45 bucks - winning! So yes sometimes literally'. You never know, if you're passing by wicked campers in Brisbane you might still be able to see my naked ass covered up by a blow up banana

Back to the point.

When you're travelling you're all on a level playing field, eating shitty cheap pasta and nicking everyone's bread from the fridge, drinking cheap booze and searching for the cheapest hostel with the biggest room, always trying to save more money for piss, and no one cared because it was about more than that, the surface level crap meant nothing.I had some of the best experiences and deepest conversations both sober and drunk during that trip.

This 4 months also gave me time to hone the one big skill that stopped me staying in school in the first place, to study human biology and become a physio or S&C coach and that was the confidence around people and complete strangers to speak, hold eye contact and become more tactile. After having helped my dad on the roof for years since age 11, i'd gotten so used to only really communicating with him or the stupid heavy ass roll of felt I was pinning down and hating life rolling, I could barely hold a conversation, let alone command a room of people in a class or do a 1 to 1 PT session. Hence quitting 6th form after my first week.

If travelling taught me nothing else, it taught me this. One cheap shitty wine or box of 'goon' is terrible in every country and there's no hangover like it. Don't drink more than 1 samsung bucket if you want to remember your following few days. Always have eyes in the back of your head in shared kitchens as trust me... They will nick your eggs, even if they're frying. And finally, no one really cares what you have to offer a room in a material sense. People value you for your unique personality traits, empathy, emotion and self awareness. If you can be you and 100% own that, people will like you, and if not, they will at least respect you.

*Why PT?*

Armed with all but none of the tools i thought i needed, i sat on the two longest plane rides of my life set on the idea of becoming a PT, why? Because the mere thought made me feel physically sick and so excited at the same time. It was like losing my virginity all over again. Just raw passion and terror and no idea of what direction to head in... haha yep we went there!

If you have ever asked the question of whether becoming a PT is a good fit for you, by the end of this book it will be clear, Hell yes or no, Simple!

But before reading on, ask yourself the question - how does the idea make you feel?
If the answer is 'yeah that'd be cool or fun' then trust me keep your membership and get your buzz that way. Because as you read on you'll soon realise without all those reserves of passion and energy, you won't even make it through your 3 month probation period in a gym.

## How The Fuck Do I Start?

Let the fun begin, or the basic modern day slavery, full piss take but you gotta do it and months of asking have i made a huge mistake here begin. Has a real ring to it right? Well if it were easy everyone would do it, so strap yourself in!

I'm going to start with my route because it's the one I know best and it's my book… Then I'm going to share with you the best tips I have in making the right decision before even signing a contract or opening a text book.

As i mentioned earlier, prior to travelling I completed my level 2 Fitness Instructor qualification, this course was 95% completed online with a 3 day long weekend spent on site in a gym and classroom being assessed with a final multiple choice exam at the end… which I also failed first time LOL. The main reason I failed was because I was a lazy twat when it came to revision and i'm also extremely bad at retaining information, so I needed to be in a classroom environment, I learnt that the hard way. Was it a great course? Not really,  but did it cover the basics I needed to be safe and effective, yes. It cost me £600 and two full tanks of petrol, decent investment when I look back at it now.

The real work started when I got back to the UK full of enthusiasm and rocking a sick tan. The first thing I did was hook back up with Bud who took me straight back in no questions, legend.He has always had my back like a dad figure really. I had my financial security sorted, number 1!

The difference was my attitude had changed. I now knew every single day i went to work that it was helping me supplement the career I actually wanted, so funnily enough that 3 months which happened to be the last 3 months of roofing, fuck I enjoyed every damn day. Jumped out of bed with my alarm, smashed every job and left happy. What I did in my spare time was hash together the most stupid CV you've ever seen, sifting through my record of achievement from high school for any extra credits or things I could use to bolster it. I even found this tip online suggesting writing on coloured paper so that yours would stand out in a pile of other CV's. I went sunshine yellow, like full on look at me Ali G shit haha. Then searched every gym, hotel health club and PT studio in Norwich to distribute it to.

The next thing I did a lot of people thought was a bit weird, but honestly (pens out) it was one of the single most important decisions of my early career. I downloaded a free one day pass for every single gym I distributed CV's to and went and used the gym as a 'prospective member'. Why? To first of all see the obvious things - the environment, equipment available, general member base and most importantly to get an understanding of what type of people were working there and how they treated members and each other. This would give me a huge insight into my competition if I were to work there, and it was also an opportunity to find out as much information about my future competitor brands in the local area, before I was earmarked as a PT'. You see, the minute I decided to fully commit to doing what I wanted to do a switch went off and I no longer just wanted to become a PT, I wanted to become a Fitness Manager, I wanted to run PT's in whichever place I worked.

*How The Fuck Do I Start?*

I wanted to work my way up the chain as high as I could without stepping away from the gym floor, and in order to do that you have to do your research and understand what and who you are up against.

It was clear after a month of trialing gyms and also not hearing a word back from any, I had to make a decision, let it go and wait or take another step forward. I chose the latter and took out a membership at the gym I received the warmest welcome from and personally saw the most potential for myself. The staff were friendly, the other PT's were motivated but not so much so that I couldn't keep up, and the members seemed very much like a great mix of potential clients and friends.

I joined up and went everyday for the first two weeks until i found out who worked when, doing what and more importantly who was the gym manager! Shaun was one of the most important people i've met in my career as a PT because that crazy son of a bitch gave me a chance. I noted the times  during the day that he might' be in the gym at the same time doing his own sessions, made general conversation, I actually found I got along with him pretty damn well to be honest. After speaking I would always ensure my sessions and movement were to the button, every rep was performed with purpose and the best technique I possessed. This would prove really important down the line.

Every time I went to the gym I asked a guy Adam a very charismatic handsome 6 foot dude, if there was a job going. Every single time. For a couple months i think he just thought i was a desperate tit, which was kinda true, i was, I wanted in badly!

But it worked because one day walking in I saw Shaun's door slightly ajar with a young looking chap inside and another looking nervous as fuck in the cafe area.

So i asked Adam again and he told me it was a receptionists job initially, to which i said i'll take it. He asked Shaun if I could get an interview, to which he responded - "can you get back here in a suit for 4:30?' "You're fucking right I can!' I went straight to Top Man and brought the best fitting suit I couldn't afford and rolled up like I was either getting a job or about to walk down the aisle.

I thought the interview was going well until he told me i was up against a sports science degree candidate fresh out of university. Great that's me fucked I thought to myself, the following question that came out was 'what do you think you have that they don't?' My honest answer was experience and drive. I'd grafted  since the age of 11 , nailed my work experience at Soccer World so much so they offered me a job, which I declined. Big up Soccer World! And the cherry on top, i'd just been travelling so i've seen the world but more importantly it meant I was settled and ready to start my career without that itchy foot setting in again anytime soon. We took a walk round the gym discussing what the role entailed etc, the deal was sealed once we entered the free weights area and started talking about training. He remembered seeing me train and referenced at that point I clearly knew what i was doing which was a huge buzz for me and offered me the job a couple days later. 3 shifts - Friday late, Saturday Late and Sunday… LATE! Otherwise known as the graveyard shifts, but i wasn't going to say no, it was a foot in the door! All three were reception and clubroom shifts with the hope that one day a fitness instructor position would open up. In the meantime, I was already working on gaining my first PT clients without anyone even realising.

Every person I swiped in daily i'd try to memorise their names as soon as possible, so upon arrival I could greet them personally. Also when i'd do my ten minute checks and walk round the gym, i'd take in little snippets of their sessions or generally just encourage with a sentence or a smile as i went past, so that next time they came in I could reference said machine or movement and say things like 'a couple extra reps on that leg press today Jim' or 'swim today Janice?' Seemingly very minor interactions but  2 years later some of these people became clients due to these initial interactions. The whole time i was doing this i believed it was just customer service 101, everyone was like this right? Caring about strangers enough to naturally want to keep their motivation and energy high, but no one else was doing it.

(Pens Out) - It's very easy to overlook the small things when passion and energy is involved. When it's all just bubbling away and you can't wait to start, that is the very moment you have to stop, step back for a second and be calm. Think about more than just the goal of becoming a PT. Don't allow yourself to be so one dimensional and short sighted with your ambition. Think about where you want to work and why, even research. The types of people you want to eventually be coaching and how you are going to gain clients. Because trust me, it's not about looking jacked or super slim and popping up a poster and wearing a smile.It's far simpler than that, it's about being human and approachable first. What makes you human and what makes you approachable? Sell that first.

It got to the point where the older ladies who would do aqua fit and even a few of the more fussy guys would ask specifically for me to make their coffee or cappuccino when they came in, at this point I knew I was doing something right even if it was just the froth on top of the cap!

Around the same time as things started to feel comfortable, my relationship with my X partner also broke down for a multitude of reasons. But mainly, I was no longer the person who walked into that night club pissed needing to feel loved. I was now starting to become the person I needed to be and unfortunately for her I needed to be selfish, I needed to focus on me. I had been spending every weekend evening working in the gym and every day  training and mingling in the gym, it was only going to end one way really.

The gloves were off, time to solely focus on work!

Finally, Shaun gave me the chance to get on the floor and start programming newbies or re-programs that no one else could be arsed to do. I programmed the arse off every single person who came to see me and told them when i wanted them to come back for a re-program to check on progress, I wasn't getting paid extra for this and at times it was an utter ball ache but again i say, start to be the person you want to become early then the transition will feel seamless down the line.

Before I talk about the next step/s i took, I really wanted to just highlight the point of visualisation, manifestation and basically faking it until you make it and just how powerful it was for me in the early days. I never had and still do not have all the answers but a book i read early on in my career called 'The Secret' by Rhonda Byrne, taught me a hell of a lot about the law of attraction. Straight up here, I'm not about tuning into frequencies, vibrations and energies etc it's just not a language that I connect with. But the basic idea of visualising what you want to become or attract into your life and approaching everyday with gratitude and belief that you already have that life is super powerful, or at least it was for me anyway. 'Be The Man You Want To Become'... from day 1 of making coffee's and signing up members during my reception shifts, I was already visualising myself in my Fitness Manager role, what my office space was going to look like and especially the systems I was going to change and bring in.'

At this time I got the opportunity to study from a government funded scheme to hit my level 3 PT. Basically if you were already in work within the industry you could get funded for your qualification. This was HUGE for me and i'm forever grateful to Shaun and Louise my course manager at Lifetime, who I qualified through for that opportunity. Queue a year of burning the candle at both ends and right down the middle. But at this point, things also started to become a little easier and a lot more fun. John had come back from travelling and I managed to get him a hook up at the gym as well. Basically we just fucked around and had a laugh most days whilst plotting how we wanted to take over the PT world and the goal was to become the biggest PT's in Norwich at that time and change as many lives along the way as we could. One thing that was extremely powerful and helpful for me in those early days was support and trust. Shaun as a manager was huge and also Ben the guy who owned and ran the whole brand. Everyone was terrified anytime he would pop in' I certainly didn't' wanna lose my job but I wanted to learn from him and the respect he had gained. He gave me a lot of time back then and that was huge for my confidence.

Also during this time i had another life changing encounter. One of the people who I would swipe in the gym 3-4 times per week anytime between 5:15 and 5:30pm was Carly, she worked at BMW round the corner, wore the sexiest tights I'd ever laid eyes on and was definitely too tall for me in heels.

I was hooked and I don't mean I just wanted to sleep with her, I was obsessed. My life goal had switched on its head from the second I laid eyes on her and suddenly started to include this woman, who didn't even know I existed. Honestly, I've asked her many times if she noticed how hard I crushed on her and for the first 3 months of me practically grafting her she never even noticed! It worked out because 10 years later we're still going strong. Hopefully she knows I exist now and I'm not just a 'Very' personal trainer haha

The Lv3 course was hard i won't lie, the step up in knowledge and information you had to not only learn but understand and be able to deliver was huge. There were many times I looked through my folder thinking I would never understand this enough to pass a practical exam or a theory! I failed the theory the first time (standard Leon) but the practical I absolutely smashed out of the park. For most people it was the opposite way round, so it was a win.

Obviously I qualified eventually..... Can you imagine, TRICK haha

But I decided to continue learning for a further year with the support of Lou and Shaun and get qualified as a Fitness/Leisure Manager and GP referral specialist as well. Neither of which were options to use right then, but I had them in place ready for when I could take full advantage.

So you're a qualified PT, what now?

# The Sobering Truth

'If you thought becoming a PT was hard you just wait until you're qualified.'

I sat there thinking I now possessed every secret, every piece of knowledge and all the understanding I was ever going to need. So I sat back and awaited the stampede of clients to run towards me.

It didn't happen

(Pens Out) What a lot of people don't tell you is that the second you become a PT in a gym you are then seen as a salesman and everyone who had taken a step or two towards you, suddenly takes a couple steps back, mainly due to past experiences.

Everyone I used to speak to now thought I was going to try to sell them sessions every time I opened my mouth. Along with that, every other PT was then acutely aware that there was fresh meat to compete with. So at this point you have a dilemma, on one hand you need to get the clients so you need to talk to people but on the other, the second you start to sell you become every stereotype they expect of a PT… well apart from the part where they presume you're shagging every client you have, ye you get that to, look forward to that one!

What I decided to do, and by no means do I think it's the only way, and upon reflection maybe not the most successful but we'll get to that. I spent about £300 practically half my months wages LOL on getting a couple of posters designed and 500 business cards made at top spec with a flash ass design and put them up on every free advertising board in the gym and slid 4 cards down the spine of the holder as well so people could just help themselves.

*The Sobering Truth*

The reason I put the business cards there was to get a rough gauge of interest in each area of the gym. I knew that just because someone picked my card up it did not mean they would call or email, but what it did tell me was that there were two key parts of the gym where people were truly engaged with my advert, enough to actually take a card away. So what did I do… spent more time walking around that area, and being on hand for anyone as and when they needed help. The downstairs water fountain and outside the sun bed rooms soon became my most successful client pick up areas in the first year off the back of that exercise. I also then knew the first place I was going to put up new posters, ads, competitions or any form of promo in the future. It may feel a pinch anal and costly as a ton of my cards went without clients coming in for sure but fast forward 2 years and I was the only PT in that gym turning over 50+ hours per week in sessions, as well as handing off clients to other professionals and taking a small commission, so I think it was worth it in the long run. It's really important to remember in the world of advertising it's not about 100% conversion rates, you will never gain 100% return on the amount of cards you put out. There are many other things to take into consideration with advertising and I think the best thing I did was look at it as a totally separate thing. Advertising was simply away of getting the message out and if people became clients after, happy days. I know if I expected that every time a card went I was swiftly going to receive a call, i'd have gotten disheartened very quickly!

In this modern world you could be easily fooled into thinking that posters are outdated and no need to hold business cards when you can just give someone your Instagram handle right? Wrong! I will let you in on a secret, as TheLeanMachines our biggest tool for our advertising part of our business still to this day… email!

Every damn person says email is dead but we are all simple and old fashioned at heart and love the retro freedom of reading emails. In fact over 5 million vinyls were sold in 2020, fucking vinyls!! And that's in an age of Spotify. Retro vibes. Just the same as I still see people sat on the tube reading their paperback books and newspapers, if I have something truly important to write, I first use a pen on paper before trusting the digital keyboards. Business cards and posters are the same and I urge every single one of you coaches out there to invest in that area of your business straight off the bat. If you're not new and don't have them, get them! It's a non aggressive simple form of advertising and also a business card is the only form of advertising you can pitch in the gym with zero effort and can leave the building and enter someone's wallet, purse or cork board back home after. Yes people still have cork boards as well… Retro!

### *Other Forms Of Advertising*
Again this is just my opinion based on my experience and things I fucked up or didn't try through ego or fear and I should've!

1.   Do free stuff and do it publicly and obviously at the start.
You will often hear me say I rarely ever give away my services for free nowadays and that's not because I'm tight or a money grabber, far from it. It's actually a mixture of two things. 1 i've been there and done it and it worked really well but you can't give everything away for free forever.

2. people don't value it as much long term. You know what it's like when you try to help a family member, you can give them all the advice in the world but they still never really listen, it's very much the same with clients if you continue to discount everything.

I learnt this in the early days of working in the gym. They used to have an annual discount on their membership of, pay up front and you get 15 months for the price of 10, pretty decent offer and worked really well to begin with but what started to happen after a few years is members cottoned on and would suddenly start coming in and asking around the time the last offer was 'whens the membership offer coming back?" they'd literally hold off paying their membership to get this deal and if it didn't come they'd get real pissed off and leave or start missing payments. It came across to me like they didn't really value the gym at true cost so it had to be discounted. Had they not been fed the deals over and over, would it have been seen differently? I believe so.

All that being said, at the start you are not focussing on any of the above it's all about foot fall, being seen is everything and the best way to be seen is to offer free stuff. A lot of egotistic coaches out there value themselves, their lv3 or pointless degree so highly that they will 'simply never discount their prices for anyone' from day one. I understand, but how do you expect to show what you can do as a coach by having zero clients? I took on as many spin classes, body pump, body combat and boxercise classes I could in the first few years. Yes i enjoyed teaching group exercise, like really enjoyed it! But there was also another reason, that a lot of coaches are undervaluing and overlooking. I was getting paid my wage to teach the class and I was front and centre with up to 30+ potential new clients with all eyes on me. That is a shit ton more than if I were to just walk round the gym for that hour. As the teacher you are there to educate, infuse and energise the member and if you can do that in a group of 30 just imagine if it were one on one?

I also held mini boot camp sessions with clients in what some would see as random or pointless areas of the gym. Next to the cafe or clubroom was an outdoor patio area which never got used. The key here is that the full length of the clubroom was glass fronted and tables lined it, captive audience! Yes it was great to get outside in the elements and really offer clients something different in their sessions but also it opened me up to a new audience. The audience that only really came in to swim, steam and have a coffee. I could teach all the classes and mince round the gym as much as I liked but they'd never see me.

The power of FREE is quite incredible but what I can not stress enough is to plan ahead and stick to your plan when it comes to free. First of all decide which of your services and for how long you will offer them for free. Think about the best way to create as much impact as possible i.e if it's a bootcamp where is the best place to do it for free, where other people will also see you. And finally decide what is NEVER going to be free, always have something of your services that will never be given up for nothing and make sure every person knows about it. For me it was the nutrition protocol and also writing more long term personalised programs, if anyone wanted that extra support they had to pay, simple.

I will say there's a form of advertising that sits piles above anything else i've mentioned though, and that's you. All these ideas of how to get seen more and increase foot fall etc all came secondary to the fact that i wanted to get to know people and understand them. Then I wanted to make training simple, approachable and less macho bullshit our industry was so full of. To be a great PT or business man/woman you must first be aware and be a good human.

I genuinely couldn't care less if someone came to every class and never became a client of which there were many, or had a reprogram with me and never came back, as long as i'd added value to them in some way and made fitness that little more fun. Morals are everything and you as a person are really important to your business, especially when you are front facing so don't forget that. I still to this day can remember practically every name of clients I've coached over the years and could probably tell you the name of a family member as well. Is that important to you? Maybe not but to me my clients were and are everything.

## Learn Your Craft
### *'Coach Who And How You Want To'*

Let's fast forward a couple years now, you have a few client success stories under your belt, you've also fucked up a couple times and got nowhere with others, it happens that's part of learning. Now you're starting (I hope) to find a bit of a pattern. People that tend to come to you and you get results for them, they all tend to have something in common. It's 50% to do with them and their efforts and 50% to do with your energy and drive to get them there. You need to understand this very early, you won't enjoy working with every single type of client you come across, it's just impossible. It's nothing against the client but some personalities or goals just won't fit with you. This is why I have a screening process now, yes there's medical areas I can't work with but also there's some people who fill out a Par-Q and i'm so damn different to them and what they want i just know i'll never get the results for them in the right way because i'm not absolutely buzzing just reading the Par-Q. Remember your clients are walking, talking and often gossiping adverts for you, so make sure they're the best adverts possible and the best way to ensure that is to find your niche.

Your niche will be a mixture of
A personality match - so you can speak and are on the same wavelength, and so the hours in the gym are not painful!
And their goals exciting you as much as them.
It might sound a little silly because your clients goals have nothing to do with you physically but you have to be interested enough to help get them there. I get so excited by every client's goals that I work with now, in a way I actually feel like they're my goals. This will help get the best results possible in the long run.

And ask yourself, could i see this client 5x per week and not want to pull my ears and eye out... Or theirs? That can sound dark and maybe a little over the top to a certain degree but too many people that I've come across over the years purely see the money. Every PT including myself loooved the clients who came in and wanted 3 or 4 sessions per week and paid for blocks up front, BOOM winner winner! But if you set your business up with just money in mind, sure you'll make a ton of cash to start with but you'll get minimal results and dread more of your work days than you can imagine, especially if you're stuck coaching someone 3x per week for the next 8 weeks and they annoy you from day one... Enjoy that buddy!

One thing that can help in establishing your niche is further education. Don't get me wrong everyone slags their PT lv3 qual off 5 years down the line when they've learnt more, established their niche and got a bit cocky but it's important to remember you'd be nowhere without that first! Picking up books and extra courses that focus on certain aspects of coaching can really help. I know many a coach who started out doing it all then 5 years down the line the only people they would work with are stage prep, then others who only work pure sports nutrition with zero face to face. A lot of this comes from education via books and absorbing information from others plus an acute understanding and grip of what they enjoy. It might seem self centred, especially if you are a PT already reading this. The industry is set up for us to simply supply a service, client puts money in hand, and we churn out sessions and training plans. But I am constantly reminding people at every stage and level that it's still THEIR business and in order to give the client the best result, they first have to enjoy what they're getting up to do everyday as well.

Far too many PT's spend all their energy and time focusing so hard on attracting clients that they forget the part where they still have the right to choose and refuse clients. I'm going to answer the next question for you, before your doubts and insecurities start screaming at you to stop expanding beyond your comfort zone.

'*What if I discover my niche and stop gaining clients or become less busy?*'

Ok so this is where you really need to trust yourself and remain focussed on what you want to achieve, bigger picture people. Paranoia sets in real fast when we are used to seeing say 30 hours of PT and it drops below 25 a few weeks in a row, and I get it, but you have options.

1- Simple but often forgotten when things are going well, advertise more or start again if you've stopped. Advertising is the number 1 most important form of consistency you need when running a business. I have two huge whiteboards up, one in my office and one in my gym and both of them have reminders written on them about the products and advertising that needs to be completed for each. And guess what? The notes never get wiped off, changed or completed, why? Because it never ends. When you're busy simply build a waitlist, it shows people want your time and gives you leads for when it gets quieter, if it gets quieter.

2- Change your price. The most ballsy thing i did as a young coach was use a supply and demand method. From 0-30 PT hours I had my standard price, beyond that the following 5 hours meant getting home late or not being able to train exactly when i wanted, so it had to be worth it. I put my price up by £5 per session.

Then for every 5 hours I grew beyond that the price went up just the same. It was a pinch unfortunate that my 50-55 hour clients were paying almost double my 25-30 as it wasn't their fault directly that they were encroaching into my free time but what they were getting because of it was 110% of my efforts as well because they paid top dollar for me and i appreciated that. It's a great model and works well in most scenarios as long as you have a reason, i.e don't just say fuck it i've got 30 clients now and start charging them all double over night including your original clients because they ain't getting any extra for that price hike and will disappear fast.

This model also picks up some of the slack if you lose a few of the original clients as you start to work towards your niche as they will be paying more to cover the difference. So i suggest once you have decided what your niche is, also decide that from the very next client who walks in, you are now charging an extra £5/10 per session from that day forward.

3- This is the scariest option and something i never needed to do but i saw some PT's do great things through this method. One of which was a really good friend of mine to this day, Matt. We worked together for a while and for a few reasons he changed the environment he worked in. When he came back he was a totally different beast as a coach after learning from other pro's, a different business model and in some areas gaining a truer appreciation for some of the comforts in our original space. A new environment, one which supports your niche better or just offers new experience. For instance if you discover your niche lays in stage prep but the average age of your current members is 65+.... You're gonna have to move or start prescribing gear to every client, haha I joke but you see what I mean!

Never be afraid to change direction. One thing I always struggled with and still do sometimes is that to change your mind or adjust your course meant that you had failed in the eyes of your peers. It's simply not the case. The only failure you should be ashamed of is the one that you never allowed to happen, because you were too scared to take action in the first place. Wanna know how I know that? Because that comes from past experience, something I can not undo now and still haunts me to this day.

I used to be a decent runner back at school representing the southern counties on track and cross country. I loved it when I was in the front pack but the second I had my first race where I got my ass handed to me, I lost the love. I originally told myself it was because I was just unhealthily competitive, which to a degree I was sure, but the real reason was that I was scared to push myself and put more effort in and still maybe not win. So i quit.

Then football, I was pretty decent at that too, (says every dad in his thirties) but I was. Captained my team for 4 years, hit county trials etc and was scouted a couple times but 16 hit and I still wasn't the next Beckham. Well shit that wasn't the plan, what do I do? At 16 it's a bit shit because every year prior to that you play under 14's, under 15's and so on, but at 16 you jump straight into under 18/19's, so some of the kids you'd be playing could be 2 years older than you. There was an opportunity for me to trial for a paid spot like £30 a game I think, but yep I bottled it. Not because i didn't think I was good enough but because i'd rather avoid it all together than to try and fail.

Final example… i really fucking took some time to learn from this one. Boxing, yep I was pretty decent at that too.

My dad was a professional boxer in the 80's and early 90's. He taught me to fight like a pro, so the first time I stepped in the ring to spar, I floored a lad with a left hook to the body. For context, amateur boxers never throw body shots. Fast forward 3 years and I'd won both fights I had, which took a while to get because of my last name alone. Everyone knew my dad and wanted their boys to win their first fights, so dodged me. I made matters worse by taking a lad for my first fight which was his 7th and won, not ideal. Anyway i was training for the novis 10's - first step towards ABA's, which would've been the end goal before GB trials. I got a bye in the first round ,then while training for the second fight i became distracted, or so i thought. Started getting pissed more and missing training etc the usual teen stuff. Got too far away from my fighting weight and quit. For a long while i blamed it on just not being dedicated enough etc but it was actually the crippling fear of ever losing a bout that stopped me. And that fear grew every single time I won.

So trust me when I say don't let that stop you, because they are the annoying things you remember down the line.

## Measuring Success And What It Means To You

Right let's talk about that crazy and addictive word - success! Be honest with yourself right now when i ask you this question;

What is success to you and what makes you successful?

And before your inner extremely intelligent ego kicks in telling you this is some form of test, it's not! There is no wrong answer here as long as it's 100% your own opinion and you own it.

As with every other chapter within this book there's a particular reason i've placed this here, and that's because i really wish it took me less time to pull my head out of my own ass along my journey. Being in the fitness industry let's be honest, for 99% of professionals, unless you are working every hour under the sun it's not what we would call a 'rich man's game'. It's all about the hustle and slow long term progression. But that doesn't stop or dull the wants and desires no no no, in some cases it can actually make it worse. If you become a PT to a pretty high earner (I had a few on my books) they are very motivational people to coach and are extremely driven human beings for sure, but they also have a lot more influence on you and your business than you might realise. I remember coaching a guy who ran a MASSIVE business for a good year or so and within 3 months of general chit chat I had decided that what I was doing with my business was not enough, I needed to expand, I needed to earn more and grow. In some ways this was not wrong but the nature and approach i was thinking up in order to create such growth would've meant sacrificing the quality and personality of my coaching by a good 50%!!

It's very easy for people to offer advice or solutions to a 'problem' you have when they are at the top looking down.

*Measuring Success And What It Means To You*

And I highlighted the word problem there because looking back it was never a problem to me within my reality, it just didn't make sense to an outsider who was used to turning over quadruple my salary and working 2 maybe 3 days per week. To that person I was not successful because my numbers in both hours worked and money in the bank did not match their ideals for success.

So before we start skipping into the next chapter which is all about that crossroads moment you face in any career, we need to start asking ourselves the question of what success really looks like to us personally. Here I am at 33 years old about to share what success looks like to me and it's honestly worlds away from where it was 3 years into PT. I by no means believe this is the end of the road for my success in business or life, i'm also 100% certain this list will change and grow as time goes on and that's really important to understand and appreciate. Often we see and except that everything changes in life but ourselves, beliefs, ideas, opinions and even direction at times must adjust and grow in order for us to. Don't be the stubborn mule stuck in their ways picking fights with the world, grow with it!

When I talk about success and what it is to me I have a list that I keep and recite to myself in times I feel myself either slightly losing my way, or generally when I have moments of prolonged want over need kick in, which happens! These help me stop, breath and focus. These are much like positive affirmations that many use.

I start like this;

'I am successful because;'

- I have a wife that loves me and i love her
- I'm a father which is present and able
- I wake up everyday day and love my work
- I need' very little in life and understand the difference between wants and needs
- I have a beautiful home
- I'm proud of myself
- I have an able body I can trust

10 years ago they would've read all about money, because at that time that was the only measure I had, that and material possessions. I understand that in order to have a beautiful home and enjoy the work I do it took years of bloody hard graft to get there, but the thing that's so easy to lose sight of is why you're doing it all in the first place.

I know (it took me a while) but I knew a fair few years ago that i didn't want to own my own gym or not right now anyway. I stopped valuing myself on just the physical transformations I helped my clients gain and worried more about how they felt in their skin along the journey. More importantly I started essentially stopping and tracking every 6-8months to assess what i was doing, if it still made me happy, and a success within my own right.

It's very easy in the PT world to feel like you have to keep chasing and for some that will always be the goal and it's never a problem if you know that's all you want, go for it.

But there's also a point where you have to stop and ask yourself, what you're doing, is it bringing value to you and making/keeping you happy. There's no point being a PT with a goal of reaching 70 hours of PT per week if you don't know what that's truly going to add to you as a person. Honestly, money should never be the prime deciding factor of success, what you're doing should be, so have a little think and try not to answer directly with money in mind, you might be surprised what comes up.

*'Always trust your gut as they say.'*

## Year 3 The Separator
### *'Commit Or Quit'*

In any job there's a time where you decide whether or not it's right for you, or if you don't someone else will decide for you instead. In PT it's no different to other careers apart from the fact that within 6months of coaching, you've already been told by every half arsed PT or X PT that it's a revolving door industry and you're likely to quit within 3 years, because you can't simply just train all day and the hours are shit bla bla bla!

I was told this at least 4 times before i'd even fully qualified so be aware of that, it will be said. But mainly be aware that it will also only be said by people who have already or nearly already quit, hopefully this book will help you avoid that fate.

I remember my '3 year itch' like it was yesterday! Admittedly mine was not the same circumstances as most of you might face, as Youtube was slowly becoming something at this point and was a secondary focus or distraction you might say. I woke up everyday for what felt like forever, it was actually only 3 weeks (i'm quite dramatic) and had the same questions spiralling around in my head constantly.

*'Is this really what i want to do for the next 40 odd years old?'*

*'Am I actually enjoying it?'*

*'Am I a decent coach?'*

*'Is this it or do I expand?"*

As I said, my circumstances were different, mainly due to the fact that I could see a whole new life happening around me through other people's eyes, and journeys. You will hear a lot more about Youtube and when it all went pop in the 'Fame And Misfortune' section, but right

now let's just say the main reason these questions were being asked at this time, mainly came down to the fact that Youtube was new and exciting at the time and some of the ball park figures being thrown around for work were utterly insane. My head wanted to take the seemingly easy route!

The thing with most self employed jobs is the fear of it all just coming tumbling down around you one day, I honestly don't believe that feeling ever goes. The bigger you get the more responsibilities you have, the bigger the risk' it won't change. So first of all, understanding that and coming to terms with it really helps.

Now let's talk about retirement 'fuck me' at 33 alright lad, i'm doing ok! But this one really gets my goat about 'can I see myself doing this for 40 years' it's like when some idiot walks up to you or comments on a post about my tattoos 'are you not worried what they'll look like when you're 60?"
Seriously if i'm 60 and still give a flying one what people think of my tattoos or lose any sleep over them myself, then i've lived life totally wrong in my opinion!

think to make a 40 odd year long commitment to anything is quite literally impossible to comprehend for most people, myself included. With my business nowadays I simply have my daily, weekly, monthly, annual goals and a 3-5 year max target. That 3-5 max target is the most changeable element as well because, well life.

I can plan as much as I like for something to happen by "said date" but things happen, wants and needs change and adapt, so must the goals and targets. Some people work differently and you may be that person who needs that 5 year plan to motivate you daily, great stick to it rigidly and you will get there. But for me if that were the only driver everything else around me would become second to that. Most super successful people I meet who live by that 5 year plan end up stinking rich but fucking miserable and alone, or nearly alone. So really think about the type of person you are when it comes to setting any targets related to work. My biggest piece of advice would be, please do not ask yourself if you could see yourself doing it still at retirement age, because the goal is to hit it so hard that you will be well sorted and retired far before you even get bored of what you're doing!

You will forever question if you are a good enough coach and even more nowadays because we're exposed to so much more content from all kinds of professionals or brofessionals as well as I call them. You can have all the qualifications under the sun but there will still be someone out there with more or someone out there who can present it more effectively than you. Another thing that will not help your self belief is the failed clients, it will happen, not a single great coach has a 100% success rate, even long after they've found their niche and work with the same type of client all the time, they will still fail and so will you! And guess how many of your failures you remember, 100% of them. So in those days where you start to question your abilities, what pops into your head? Old David who just couldn't seem to shift the weight! You have walking talking failures there to constantly remind you and lead you to question yourself, it's quite frustrating really when you think about it!

The final one on here that will answer all of the above questions for you in my opinion, is this little thing we call Imposter Syndrome. You know that feeling that someones gonna catch you out at some point and you're just winging it no matter how many quals you have.Every person I meet whose 'living their best life' in the career they love, they all have this feeling that someones coming, this is too easy, it's fun even. Someone surely has to turn up and slap me down at some point.

I've observed it in myself and many others and I think it's a small sign that you are doing what you are truly supposed to be. We are brought up with this disillusion that work is and should be nothing but hard and we're really not supposed to enjoy it most of the time. Sure it has really hard times and areas that are not particularly that fun, granted. But when you're doing the right job for you, more often than not it flows quite nicely in a rhythm that fits you.

I even have this in my personal life and if i'm honest I think it's a huge contributing factor to why me and my wife have been together for 10 years. There's barely a day that goes by where I don't think at least once in the back of my head 'what the fuck is she doing with me?' or 'at some point she's gonna wake up and realise i'm an immature twat and be gone.'
Some may see this as purely a lack in confidence or self worth on my behalf... Trust me I don't struggle in those areas. I think it's just a constant reminder to truly appreciate what I have in my life. The fear of becoming overly complacent or lazy in my relationship terrifies me, so maybe it's a protection mechanism, time will tell I guess.

If you're at the 3 year stage asking all these questions, then this should really help.

First let's answer the question of why 3 years in the PT world seems to be the norm.

For most people there's almost a right of passage in the PT world like most other careers i'm sure. We become qualified thinking we know everything, realise we know nothing, graft to learn more, realise we still know nothing, then what.

Quit?

So you've done the graveyard shifts and wiped down enough stinking sweaty equipment to last a lifetime. You've probably heard far too many personal secrets about far too many of your clients that you could never look their family or close friends in the eye if you were to see them on the street. And you've probably had a handful or great clients that have become friends in the process of coaching them. But

do you know what most PT's do not do in those first 3 years? Start

thinking and planning, what's next! At this point whether we like to admit it or not, it's fucking easy right?! You're in a comfortable position with a steady flow of clients (I hope) all the equipment you should ever really need and you have a pretty cushty set up with paying your monthly gym rent or working a free shift then taking whatever else you earn home. It's really, really hard to take the next step in our industry because every-thing we know is under that roof and has been spoon fed to us in a way to make us feel dependent.

I remember sitting down trying to rack my brain as to how I was going to progress my business before the rise of Youtube and the simplest idea (emphasis on simplest here) and most logical idea that honestly came into my mind was this.

In order to take my current 50+ PT session per week business to the next level I now have to create my own gym space that rivals this one, maybe even go a little bigger. Fuck me!! Big dreams lad and your

pockets must be as deep as the med' to get that done! Secondary to that idea was to shoot high for a celebrity client list and travel to London a few days a week to achieve it and essentially start again. But, I had a new stunning relationship with my now wife that luckily I valued immensely.

It seems totally insane to think that they were the only options that came into my head but when you're surrounded by a single environment for a long enough period of time you start to think quite literally and I'd become such a part of this space that I started to believe it was the space that made me a great coach, not the delivery. Man still had confidence issues and a tasty portion of imposter syndrome it would seem ey.

The answer here is very simple but takes a hell of a lot of self control in order to do it. When you find yourself in this position as a coach or in any job in fact, the first thing you need to do is stop and assess before taking a single step further forward or away from the industry.

The fact is the ground lays completely differently to what it did 3 years ago when you had nothing but a piece of paper and a ton of enthusiasm.

You are now by no means the complete package but you've cleared level 1 and you need to decide what you want from lv2, what it's going to cost both financially and personally in time and social life etc. Only then can you truly plan ahead. Upon reflection, if I'd not headed towards the social media world my 'educated' next step would've been to employ a fresh new hungry PT to train and shadow in my spare time to bring up to my standard then funnel clients his or her way and just take commission. (I'd started doing this low key). Along with that I would have aimed to get my face in a completely new gym in the city for one day per week to start building a client base under a new roof. This is a ballsy and sometimes hard strategy as each gym can get a little pissed that you are in another competitor's space, but as long as you are straight up, pay your rent and don't go in and take clients from one gym to another you should be grand!

For me the approach was all about spreading the brand and my word further, whilst still maintaining a high standard. By training someone up, not only would it free my time up to be in another space advertising my brand, but i'd be able to help a fresh new kid in this sometimes harsh selfish industry get off to a running start. Maybe changing their perception of what the industry is so commonly known as, but also they'd still be associated with my brand via PT kit or Logo's, so again more free advertising.

In order for your business to grow and expand you have to understand and appreciate that you can't do everything and I think this is why so many PT's quit in that strange 3 year place. Because they are full or close to full, losing all of their social life due to the totally unsociable hours for sessions - mainly being around everyone else's work hours, but still wanting to be the face and in control of everything.

It simply can not happen, something has to give. Whether that be bringing someone else in, raising prices and trimming the fat a little or making the decision to step off the gas a pinch and regain some of your time back.

This is an option we've not covered yet and not because it's a wrong or weak option but because it takes a lot of clarity and self awareness to make this an option and I believe you may need a few more years to get an informed decision. But many PT's i've met have said and I quote 'I will be more than happy to have 30 sessions per week with a small active waitlist of clients, and have my weekends to myself.' That's the goal! And if that is your goal do not feel pressured to give more of your time away as you will end up resenting your work. I will say, prepare to feel resistance or pressure from external sources and people around you to 'do more' or 'want more' because that's just how so many people are wired.

It seems to me that if you are here you may have a lot to think about, so let's leave it there for now.

## It Was All Going So Well...Too Well

That fourth year, once you've made your decision to stick with it and you start to focus on your niche area, THE FUN BEGINS. I was even more hungry to do what I was doing, everyday had more purpose, energy and far better results. But what i also had, which I didn't quite understand until it all came tumbling down around me, was a LOT more responsibility and upon reflection a lot more than i could really handle alone if i'm honest.

My niche happened to be working with the clients that people, including doctors and physicians had either written off all together or other coaches didn't feel comfortable either personally or professionally to get involved in. Probably should've asked myself why at that point really. But I maintain to this day, I never for a second regret working with a single person as a coach and many of the people I will mention helped me become the coach I feel I am today.

So what type of people are we talking about? I started off with a client who became a good friend of mine tbh, i'd programmed her a few times over the years between her uni studies and back n forth etc, but one year she came back and was hauntingly small. As in, the whole gym looked at her in a way that i can't even imagine how it feels to be looked at. She'd lost about half her body weight and was not overweight in any way prior, so she was now tiny! She had anorexia and was in a very bad way. As a level 3 PT even with the GP referral qualification you don't have the clearance to specifically 'treat' Anorexia and I was well aware of that.

But while everyone got really caught up in the physical and mental illness, I looked at the person and saw a human being who loved training, needed to get physically stronger and most importantly was very intelligent. So if anyone was going to get through to her, it sure as shit wasn't going to be a family member saying 'you need to eat' or a doctor giving a second rate food plan and setting goals like 'try and challenge yourself to eat a Mc Donalds this week!' You are fucking kidding me right? And that was legit a challenge set to her! So I said I would take her on and help, but only with the full backing of the gym and also full time contact with the family to which thankfully everyone was happy and onboard.

I remember the first day i walked round the gym with my PT T-shirt on and putting this chronically Anorexic client on a leg press machine, the looks I received are some of the most awful looks i've received as a coach. People were furious and even made their worries known to receptionists. From an outsider's perspective I get it, you see a PT seemingly training' a client who is massively underweight and presume it's from a body fat perspective or aesthetics right, fair but wrong! Our initial sessions were 15 minutes long and consisted of 3 sets of 5 slow reps on a leg press, followed by some yoga based stretches, and more importantly, a chat about absolutely anything other than the condition. You see this client was obsessed with training and being in the gym, that's how she got into this position in the first place. But I knew she was an intelligent person who would've known that, so also would've thought to stop if she could or truly wanted to. I knew straight off the bat that the gym HAD to stay if we were going to recover, but I was the one who moderated how much gym, how long the sessions were and exactly what we would focus on, that was the deal.

We worked well together making little deals along the way of 'you hit X weight by X date and we can add in X movement or add minutes to your session.' I remember how much she really wanted to go for a run, this became a huge bargaining chip down the line.

It went very well with monthly weigh-ins performed on Boots scales, so that any worry I had was taken away as there were more metrics shown on the screen than a simple text saying X weight. She brought in her print off receipts from the machine every time and I could track the progress but could also very much see it physically as well. Trust and respect is key in this story much like with every other client but being brutally honest was also key, she knew why i had her weigh there, because I needed to be sure and her knowing that was the truth and real reason was enough. We obviously focussed lots of our conversation time on nutrition education - as in macros, calories, the why the what's and the how's. Not just eat this because it has X calories, it was understanding and learning what each food group did and would offer to her performance and growth. As we always say - knowledge is power! And now she probably has more knowledge in the nutrition world than me as she continued to learn more and more far after recovery. If you could see her now... jeez!!

Due to the success of this client, I naturally attracted a lot of attention in this area from people who seemed to be struggling through the NHS protocol. Fast forward a handful of success stories and full recoveries, a client came in and worked with me but also went to their next NHS group meeting and told the therapist that she was also working with me alongside the treatment.

I 100% wanted that and believe to this day the NHS protocol is fantastic and works, but those guys and girls are overwhelmed daily by the amount of people they have flooding their doors, all I was there for was to give the individual that little more support they might need, or so i thought. This client was told abruptly 'if you're working with him you can't have support from us too! He's unqualified and irresponsible and works against what we're trying to achieve here!' hmm which is? I thought. The client thankfully told them to do one and came and told me what was said and by who... que the ballsiest play i've ever made as a coach! I decided to contact said professional and asked for a face to face meeting. Not for an argument or dick swinging competition but to put a face to the name that was slagging me off and maybe at least be able to find a middle ground where we could work together silently to help people. At this point I had a 100% recovery record whereby every client who I had worked with had both an obvious jump in recovery rate within weeks of working with me and had not relapsed, so it made sense. The meeting went terribly and I was essentially talked down to by a doctor who I knew simply hated me before I walked in the door. I also knew i wasn't going to change their opinion on me so i left it with

'well i just wanted to put a face to the name you've been so happily slagging off, and wanted you to know that i'm not some juiced up PT thinking he has all the answers or under playing the seriousness of the condition (hence asking for the meeting). Nor do I believe I'm better than you. I just want to help people and I thought that's what you wanted too, I was clearly wrong!'

'BALLS OF STEEL!'

When I look back now there was no way i could've got her onboard. I was under qualified and if anything ever went seriously wrong, it came down on her not me, so i don't take offence now... unlike then LOL.

After this, I continued to make myself and services available to vulnerable people from all areas, not just ED's.

The biggest case I have ever worked on was a guy, very fit guy in fact with a couple kids who'd come in and smash the treadmill with 5 and 10k runs most nights of the week no problem. The staff gave him the nickname David Beckham because he was a spit! Suddenly no1 saw him for a month or so, then the news dropped. He had gone to the doctors complaining of headaches and left with the diagnosis of a brain tumour in a very awkward place, at first it was seen as inoperable due to the risk of life but he wanted it done so had the operation, it went well but what was left of him was unrecognisable. He left the hospital wheelchair bound, with practically full left hand side paralysis from limbs to facial muscles, blind in one eye and also very hard to understand when he spoke due to the lack of jaw muscular control. He was told this would be it for the rest of his life, that he would never walk again! He was even told the wonderful words 'you should be grateful and happy to be alive after the op' Fuck my that would send me over the edge with rage! To me I thought this was the biggest blow he could've taken, but it wasn't. He went from being a very hands on dad and very active to suddenly realising he couldn't be fully left alone with his young children and guarantee their safety every again.

Nor could he pick up and carry his daughter around anymore. This killed him and I believe this was what made him even step foot back in the gym.

After the family had a meeting with the gym manager to explain where he was at and to get permission for him to use the gym again etc I just watched him in the gym. What happened next I can honestly say was the best decision and the start of the most fulfilling journey of my career. I knocked on Shaun's door and basically said I've no idea what to do or where to start with the guy but I want to help. Whether I am essentially his chaperone for the time in the gym so his wife can drop him off and have a break or I can get him walking again I will do it. I don't want to be paid because it's so far out of my remit I can't even pretend I will have a protocol, but i just can't let that be his reality.

Luckily he and his family said yes.

We started in the pool due to him not being able to stand and balance alone, using floats to help with balance and coordination. I won't go into the depth of the coaching the what, why's and how's but what I will say is 9 months later we completed a 2 kilometre totally unaided walk to the gym with his backpack on from home. That basically meant he could be self-sufficient again and get to and from the gym by foot if needed, a big deal for a proud man!

Don't worry i'm not going to sit here reeling off all my past success stories... it'd be a long book if I did, eyyyy!
But just to build a picture of how I ended up down this path and what led me to a client that almost cost me my career...

At this point I was dabbling with online coaching, mainly due to a lot of people contacting me from all over via my Facebook page after hearing about some of the success stories etc. With little experience in this field I just dived straight in and quickly found myself working with 5 or 6 long distance clients, all your standard clients. Then came my first enquiry

from a person who had mental health issues, or said that they can sometimes struggle with their mental health etc

Leon being Leon thought - that's fine we will screen and if nothing comes up too big of a deal then we will crack on and work with the person, not the history. MISTAKE.

This client went from being someone who came in asking for nutrition support and a couple days of gym programming, to what ended up being a person with borderline personality disorder and flipping on me big time.

A month of standard coaching went by and all seemed to be going well, then I received a message out of the blue questioning me in a really big way for no apparent reason. I was called a thief, a liar and a phoney in the space of the next 48 hours. I jumped on a call to ask what the problem was, and the abuse just escalated and continued for the following week. At this point I made contact and said basically i'm done! I'd coached for a month and clearly they were not happy with the result, so cool let's part ways. But it didn't stop there, she continued to come after me saying she had reported me to REPS (The PT governing body) to get me struck off, and was going to the police, like it got messy! The only option I had left to try and diffuse the situation was to give her the money back for the coaching we'd done.

So I did, with a stern email letting her know I had sought legal advice to defend myself if this were a matter that ended up in court.

The following day I was asked if I could simply 'jump on a quick call for a chat' in a language that seemed as if nothing had ever happened. So I did, with full defences in place but the phone call was calm, relaxed and in a word - normal. She explained to me that she had been struggling again since starting the training i.e that essentially triggered
her mental health instead of helping , even though she had originally said training was the only thing that helps, but hey. Then she flipped out again and was convinced my role was to take her down and destroy
her. It was hard to make sense of it all at the time but we parted ways amicably. That scar cut me deep and to this day I have never forgotten the sleepless nights, worry and stress that came from it.

I had become complacent, not through greed or ego but through trying to run my business with my heart instead of my head.

(Pens out) To be a great PT you have to discover the right mix of each ingredient to add to the pot for your clients. You have to be hard but not too hard, you have to be nice but not too nice. You have to empathise but not so much that you can't encourage change. It can be very hard at times to wear all these different hats. But in my history the greatest successes and failures as a PT for me have come from one and the same thing, caring. I care about absolutely everyone I work with to a level I'd open my front door to them anytime if they struggled and I'm ok with that and totally understand the risks that are associated with being that way now.

Some coaches leave it all at the door and couldn't tell you the names of their clients, partners or kids, or even remember their jobs. That's not a problem either as long as you know the type of coach you are and want to be, along with the positives and negatives that come with it.

## Social Media
### *Fame and misfortune*

Right let's talk social media, how to use it for business and generating leads, best ways to use each platform and also how it can fuck up your life if you get it wrong.

A little insight into the latter, slightly more dramatic one there! As i said around the 3-4 year transitional period as a coach, mine and JC's Youtube channel TheLeanMachines started to take off. We were creating content like a well oiled machine, was the biggest UK Fitness double act around and had been signed to an incredible agency who got us work from some top brands in our field, and still continue to do so to this day.

At this point we also signed a book deal with a publisher, just to add context, every fucking social media influencer or Youtube star was writing a book and getting paid insane amounts of money to do so, so we were reluctant, to say the least. I hated writing and couldn't bear the thought of spending the next 6 -9 months writing a book, plus WTF do we talk about that people are gonna want to read. It wasn't like we had millions of subscribers and fans falling at our feet, we just had an established audience who loved watching our content. Thankfully the publishers had watched us and one of them was actually a fan of the channel so they came in with a very strong concept idea for us to build from, so that's it we're writing a book then!

This also gave us the financial security to dive in head first with Youtube and just see what happens, quite an exhilarating time in my life, as well as very stressful. But that was it. We were slowly becoming full time social media and Youtube guys and slipping further away from face to face PT, until we got to the point where we had to completely stop as we spent more time out of the country than in it.

Literally at one point we flew from UK- New York - LA - UK then about 2 days later I flew out to St Lucia with the wife, back, then we flew to Universal...FML and it was all work LOL... work! This is when it started to happen for me I think, I mean the part where i started to lose grip of myself and reality (dramatic) but still very true and a hard and embarrassing thing for me to talk about. Along with a lot of cool opportunities coming in, we also started to mix with a lot of very VERY well known Youtube and Social Media people. At this point we had maybe 250,000 subscribers, very solid number but we would stand at a bar having a drink with people whereby the minimum standard was 1million plus, like some of these people were getting more views per video and uploading daily than we had total subscribers! At this time numbers were absolutely everything and we'd go to events where people would not talk to you before checking out your profile and seeing your numbers. I literally would walk up to a group of people where maybe I knew one or two to say hello, whilst I spoke to those 2 the other 3 would be on their phone searching my channel to see if we had enough subscribers to bother even interacting with. You may sit there and disbelieve this now because it just sounds crazy but it's true, some influencers back then were utter self entitled arse holes, not all but some! There's still plenty around today but luckily the world slaps them down a little more now than back then.

With all this 'influence' around me I saw a lot of what I could have if we just grew more. And it's easy when you're sat there still not owning your own home trying to find your feet and some sweaty 20 year old is talking about his properties - 'ties', it's hard not to want a bit of that.

Over the next couple of years I got far too obsessed with numbers, as in views, subscribers, comments, follows the lot. Anytime it went in the wrong direction or a video would not perform how I expected, I was miserable for days!

More embarrassing than that was the way in which I allowed other far bigger Youtube people to treat me. I never expected people to feature me on their channel or send subscribers my way but I wanted to learn from them. How do they do it, what are they filming on and what's going on in their heads day to day to stay so creative. Through this process I naturally became friends with a large number of people who would simply just take and take. I'd be writing training plans for some that would never do a day, giving out constant free nutrition advice and sharing videos and comment on them all to help them push content further etc. But there was always this overwhelming feeling of being kept at arm's length no matter what. I think that was made clear when every single time you'd simply drop someone a call, they would never answer the phone but reply to a text 5s later. If you can avoid a phone call and can't be arsed to ever speak on the phone then it's not really a friendship in my opinion.

I felt myself becoming this try hard lad constantly feeling like i had to prove myself to these people in whichever way i could. Like I was inferior because my channel and numbers were smaller, crazy! This had a good grip on me.

For many reasons my wedding was such a great time and a huge reality check in many ways as myself and wife threw it as a surprise 30th birthday. Invite everyone to a big birthday party, tell them there will be a special guest at X time so be here before then 'surprise wedding BOOM! What happened was quite interesting though. We invited all of our friends, family and Youtube and social media friends to the day as well. I almost did it like a life cleansing test really! If you have people in your life who can not be arsed on your birthday with a free bar, Nandos doing the food (yes Nandos I know) and a special guest appearance without good reason, then they're probably not the right people to keep around long term.

Guess how many of my so called Youtube friends turned up? 4 maybe 5 out of about 30/35 people who were invited. And do you know the response I got just days after the wedding 'whattt? If i'd have known it was a wedding I would've come!' That's the whole point mate... I know everyone will come to your wedding, like they are obliged to, even if they can't stand the idea of it, wedding invites have WEIGHT. But the question wasn't that, it was will they simply come to give you their time and hang out just because they care? The answer was NO and it only would've been a yes if I had 2-3million subscribers I assure you that, then there's value and most importantly content to be had.

I'm not bitter nor angry with anyone from this time, I'm actually extremely thankful because had this not happened i'd probably have lost myself even more just trying to please these people and be focusing on the wrong things still today.

*Social Media*

After this I took a different strategy with social media with a more structured approach to safeguard myself. Basically the blinkers were off!

If i'm 100% honest before I start giving my advice, I don't believe me and JC have ever really 'cracked' the social media thing. I'm not saying we're bad at social media at all, we have a damn career based around it so we do ok. But in order to really hit it big on social media it comes with the same type of approach as with PT only a lot more tiring and relentless. You have to wear many capes, normally a slightly different cape for each platform as well, so it's not like back in the day where you could effectively upload the same content everywhere and it would fly, now you have to think about the audience and behaviours of said audience on each platform. Run a rigid consistent schedule on each and constantly reinvent yourself. By no means am i saying we couldn't do that and smash a million followers on there because i truly believe we could but, remember we have been on social media for upwards of ten years. Been punched pillar to post by all platforms and realised as much as you feel in control and it's working, one algorithm change and poof all momentum gone. Quite honestly it's just not good for my motivation or mental health to give anymore to it now than i already do.

Also as well, there is a need to for want of a better word exaggerate one's message online. Whether that be via sounding a little more aggressive or abrupt in order to shock the audience into staying, or as simple as over doing the delivery and acting happier or full of energy even when you're not feeling it. This is something me and JC have always been bad at, we will create when it feels right and honest and that's it.

That being said i think it can be your strongest arm when building a PT business if that's what your goal and focus is on social media. I also believe hence why I'm putting it at this stage in the book, it will be a lot more effective once you've established your niche and direction. That way you have your identity already and all you need do is share it with the world. That being said I believe in the new world of PT and business the first thing everyone now does is create their business pages and start uploading. This can't hurt as long as you don't pigeonhole yourself too early on in the game.

Let's take a look at each platform individually because honestly that's how I want you to start thinking of them straight off the bat. Social media is not only extremely different in it's functionality but also very different in the way people consume content and engage overall. Now it's no longer just your escapism for 5/10mins here and there it's like a new email folder for you! Also do not start feeling really overwhelmed here by the amount of different platforms and thinking you need to master them all, shit some of them I am logged in and have not refreshed my feed in months because quite simply I see very minimal value there but still 'just incase' it's good to have the name handle if it flips down the line!

*DISCLAIMER- Because I also know just how fast social media moves, I wrote this in 2020 so any young bucks thinking 'what is Facebook?' haha, chill out!*

## FACEBOOK

The OG of modern day social channels. Facebook is a solid platform and has been around for years, it's not perfect in the fact that you pretty much HAVE to spend money in order to be seen by anyone other than your friends. But that being said i think it's still a fantastic arm to use. It costs absolutely nothing to create a business page and you can send it to everyone you know asking them to like it. Which if they do it gets shared to all their friends who you may not know, who see  it and also share and so on. Great way to get the initial numbers in, but and this is a big but - remember who your audience is and always think about the clients (your niche) you're trying to attract, they are NOT your family or close friends for the most part. They are simply your cheerleaders, so don't waste your energy trying to convert those into clients.

Facebook's backend paid add tool is unlike most other platforms i've ever used. Quick disclaimer I very rarely use FB adds now, through being a bit lazy but by the time this book is being read by you, I will have an annual budget assigned monthly purely to FB, that's how much value I think it can add. But if you create an add and want to put spend behind it. Not only can you decide the amount you spend and get back average reach and engagements rates for your investment. You can also tailor your ad to people in certain areas or categories along with age groups and this way you're not simply just pissing in the wind as they say. I think this platform is better for product based sales with a singular transaction i.e a training plan or kit, otherwise using it as an amplifier to get your face and brand out there more. I've not seen a ton of physical clients come from FB but a lot of sales to be made in other areas so always worth having.

# INSTAGRAM

Now, Instagram is a funny one and I will say straight off the bat it's my favourite but… only when you get to a certain size that is. So in order to use Instagram effectively for business you have to separate it from your personal life very quickly, I suggest having two accounts, 1 for friends and family etc then a second which is purely your business account. Why? Because we all still wanna see what our friends and family or idols etc are up to, so with a personal account you can scratch that itch, plus once your business one becomes big enough you don't need to keep following friends on that one to keep them happy. A business instagram account should be set up like this, it starts with who you follow and it's not the same as your personal. On here I suggest following a cross section of your industry, people doing great things, maybe even the things you'd like to do yourself. Follow editors if your editing isn't up to scratch, follow marketing experts if you think their knowledge will be valuable and most importantly follow your closest rivals, why? Because they will sure as shit be following you and watching every move to try take your ideas as soon as you drop them, so do the same and learn from them and everyone around you.

Think of your page as your shop front and your stories as the first row of clothes the customer sees as they walk in. It sounds really strange but in order for people to walk in the door, the shop needs to look great and most importantly, obvious in what it's selling. There used to be this fucked up annoying thing called 'themes' that everyone used to go by on their grid posts.

So for instance some people would only upload photos that had everything other than themselves totally white 'white theme', it seemed stupid to me and made no sense at all but as a shop front people knew exactly what they were getting, it looked clean and inviting and if you like that kind of thing like 'The White Company' for instance, you're likely to walk in the door. With Fitness it's slightly different, your theme in my opinion should relate back to your niche as much as humanly possible. If you are Mr/Ms HIIT workouts, make sure every workout or swipe workout you post is HIIT related. You may think numbers are king but there's no good having 100,000 yoga lovers following you when you are trying to sell HIIT training plans right, it's all about quality over quantity here so start thinking like that quickly. Don't try and be a jack of all trades here just keep it simple and get people in the door. If they like what they see they may follow and start saving your workouts in order to refer to them down the line, fantastic stuff as what you can do here is start to see a trend in the type of workouts people are most engaging with… create more and put them on the most popular days. This in itself is a very simple way to create a theme for your content and give people days and times to come back and look for your workouts. It's like the old school TV guide, we used to randomly watch the odd new thing but once we liked what we saw we also wanted to know when the next episode was on so we could plan ahead, content is no different.

Stories. As I said above, imagine your customer has walked through the door and now wants to know a little bit more. Remember at this point you DO NOT have the right to start slamming sales pitches down people's throat, you have to earn that. Let people get to know you, understand who you are away from  the workouts, what you eat, what you like to do and generally what you're up to day to day as well.

I love instagram stories because it's raw, unplanned and playful, so use that to express yourself.

So here's why I said that I love it. Once you get to a certain size, (you have to graft to get to 10k followers there's no two ways about it, so graft.) what happens then is you get the ability to add direct swipe up links to your stories. I love these for two reasons. One the people who do not want to purchase from you can simply not swipe up and continue enjoying your stories and main feed walking in and out of your shop as much as they like, no harm done. The other people who want to know more and by swiping up have now essentially walked up to you in your shop and asked you 'do you have this in a 7' or something like that haha. People have directly engaged with you, they've asked you a question directly. So this is where you have your website or online shop with all your products, services and more importantly prices and contact details for anyone who wants to buy. You can keep prices of PT etc private at this point and ask them to email for details, this is common as it stops competitors seeing your prices and just simply aiming to undercut yours, trust me it happens!

It's funny because if you're reading this having just scrolled through Instagram for years thinking everyone was just sharing their photos living their best life you might be a little shocked that it has so many layers of business behind it. But just to be clear, we don't put up stories everyday with a hidden agenda playing this character and all we want is your money, not at all. The fact is when I have a product I wish to sell I make it very clear and simple in stories and if people don't want it they just walk on by. Just be honest and upfront and don't try to pull the wool over people's eyes and you will do great through instagram.

## EMAIL

I LOVE EMAIL. You would not have got me saying those words a year ago trust me. But i honestly believe if it were not for writing emails ⅔ times per week for the past year i'd never have had the balls to write this book. I saw no value in putting my energy into such an old school method until IFS 2019! It was the first year of the new fitness summit on the block with all the top kids in the industry there to talk, get pissed and have a laugh. Myself and JC were hosting the main stage and we had a ball. We also got the added bonus of being able to listen to a lot of our piers talks for free. One of which was an incredible talk about email marketing with Paul Mort. A friend and someone I have a hell of a lot of respect for, so make sure you check him out if you've not already. He went off on one and by the end of this 60minute chat (which was supposed to be 45) I had made enough notes in my phone to bring out the first chapter in this book on emails alone haha

But at the end he had a pitch, his 6 week email domination course for £600 so half price. We had to know more, so said fuck it and ordered it there and then and it was not a mistake! I followed the course and started writing emails 3x per week and using a swipe up in instagram stories for people to join the free email list. Within 3 months i'd made back that investment through online coaching clients coming in alone! What email gives you the ability to do is talk openly in a relaxed environment away from the noise of social media. James Smith described it incredibly before and he says this. Instagram and other social platforms are like a dance floor, everyones out there peacocking trying to get laid. But in order for that to happen, or even maybe get a cheeky number we have to get people, off the dance floor so we can have a proper chat and get to know each other, to see if it's worth it.

That's where email comes in, we can have a chat, it's open and you can reply, purchase or just enjoy reading the dribble I put out every week. Either way there is always a P.S at the end.

The P.S is not a must but for me it's always a quick reminder of, I hope you enjoyed what i had to say and if you'd like to work with me this is how you can do it. Simply take it or leave it situation. I'm not into the whole hard sale way of doing business, I have always said I will never beg for your custom but i'll go over and above if you want it!

So if you're not sending emails I strongly suggest starting.

TWITTER
Twitter as crazy as it sounds is really quickly becoming out of date for many areas of business. A big argument for the Twitter lovers is that you can directly message anyone including celebs if that's your goal without any filter, fantastic. But one thing i've also observed a lot is that even though it says it's celeb X and they're verified etc a lot of people are paying people a LOT of money to run their social media nowadays and pre write all of their tweets, posts the lot and all they have to do themselves is sign it off with yes or no. I get it they are busy and I'm not saying everyone does that, but it does happen. With twitter I always say use it quite obviously to gain  traction for your message. You can select quotes that directly echo your message and share them daily or weekly if you so wish. You can only tweet when you have a new product or service that you're talking about and just add a link and leave it, nice! Or you can be a little more out there and ballsy with it and tag certain people in to try get their attention if you so wish.

Twitter is a game of chance, you might get noticed there and that's great, but do I think it's going to help you build your PT business? No, because to be a great PT it's about also being personal i.e having a face and Twitter tends to hide that face behind words.

I'm going to leave the whole social media chat there. Yes I have missed plenty and i'm very aware of that. Two reasons, one I may not have used it over a long enough structured period of time to be able to honestly measure it's value i.e linkedin. Or it's for a much younger audience and believe it's more about dick pics and show offs… I won't mention platforms but...you know haha

Ultimately when it comes to social media there has to be a structured agenda and valid reason for using them in my opinion. There is a huge pressure to have coverage across all areas on social, mainly through the fear of missing out, this is why I have accounts across all. But do I choose to use them all? No. Because in order for your business to be successful, you are best to spend your time mastering the delivery across one or two places (the ones that gain you the most direct work) than spreading your already thin time across all platforms just to keep up with the cool kids.

The final point to remember with all social media when it becomes a business tool as well, sometimes you will have to and should also expect to 'pay to play'. I'm honestly embarrassed to say that it took until nearly the end of 2020 before going to JC and saying 'look we need to run Facebook and Instagram ads, take control of it and crack on.' Some may say it's great that you never needed them up until then or what's the point they don't get as much engagement, but the point of ads and media spend is visibility! Think of every single person on social media creating content and sharing it all on a level playing field. Now imagine that playing field is completely submerged under water and all the potential new people are above that water line. How do you get there?

Number one that obviously breaks the surface is numbers, celebrities and blue ticks but beyond that what can you do but just create more content? The algorithm as i've mentioned before constantly changes and decides what it favours and how people view your content, and sometimes you just have to except that in order to break that waterline spending a few quid will help in the long run if enough people see you.

And it does work, i'm now the proud owner of a sealing tool for any mastic job from a dam add I skipped 10 times on Instagram that came up. On the 11th I watched it whilst taking a sip of coffee, followed the link and it arrived 48hours later. Boom!

## Reincarnation

Honestly, I love how over dramatic some of my chapter titles sound. I want to talk to you about failures, fuck ups and moments where you look back and think hmmm ye that was stupid. I'm going to sound a bit like a father in some areas here and maybe a bit deep and hippy in others, so I apologise in advance but this is really important.

If you've been in the industry for a while you've also fucked up a few times by now. If you've been coaching for say 5 years and not had a single failure or oops moment I suggest pushing yourself a little harder or find some clients with more challenging goals. I've been told by many guru's or other pro's in my field (as I'm going to say to you) to fail often and sometimes fail hard because that's where we truly grow. Had i not been through this a few times myself I never would've understood it and appreciated it as much as I do now. Like that huge fuck up with the client that almost sued me, to look at that on a surface level people would say 'christ i'd do anything to avoid that situation' but had that never happened to me i'd probably have continued working with people that I was under qualified to do so, just because my passion to help outweighed my boundaries and at some point i'd have ended up in a much worse situation, i'm 1000% sure of that.

What a lot of people are never taught is what it means to fail and what to do next to make sure you never have to repeat the same behaviour again.

Ok, imagine you are in a position whereby you have properly fucked it and it's totally out of control. Let's use an example to make it easier.

As a PT it's going really well for you and you're turning over around 40k a year, life is good. You decide based on the surface level numbers such as rent, kit hire and the number of current clients you have/need to take on a property and start coaching out of it. You take on the lease for two years but 3 months in you realise that you are

running at a huge loss, but why? I'm turning 3k a month and my

overheads are £1,500 this should be fine? What you didn't account for is the cost of electricity, music licensing, property insurance and kit

maintenance. Along with the fact that not all of your clients followed you and you are now having to spend more on advertising to get new ones in (more cost). This example escalated quickly and deeply right? Because I'm using a real life example i've seen and heard about before. They ended up having to pay around a thousand pound per month for nearly 2 years on a building they didn't use because they couldn't afford to keep

the lights on. Absolutely brutal contract I know, but that's a huge FUCK UP if you ask me. How shit would you feel the day it dawns on you that you've not only made a huge mistake, but you're also going to be paying

for it for the next year or so as well? There's many people, myself

included, who would just want to curl up in a ball and wait for a hand to pull them out. There's also people who would give it all up, go redundant and write it all off to avoid the stress, that my friend is the definition of failing. Not the act that got them there in the first place. In this position it can be hard to be logical and also very easy for me to chat about how i'd approach it from here I know, but still. Once the shit hits the fan with every fuck up there is always a sense of calm during the storm, where if

you catch it just right you can gain some real clarity. At this point it's very important to first be nothing but thankful for what's happened, twisted right?

But if you can't look at a situation for the lesson, even if you don't know what that lesson is yet, you've already quit. Would you ever have understood or realised how much it truly costs to not only get the lights on but run a successful space had this not happened prior? Some will say do your research in the first place and this is granted, but for the sake of this example say you hadn't. Before you even take your first step in trying to sort this situation you are now acutely aware of the exact cost of running your own spot and if in the future you decide to do this again, you will have that knowledge.

After the initial appreciation for the first lesson it swiftly moves to lesson number 2, 'how do I get out of this situation in a positive way?' emphasis on the positive here, it's not about just surviving a failure that helps you grow, it's being able to turn it into a positive that's really important. You start by accepting the inevitability of it, what parts of the recovery are inevitable? Well here it's simple due to the contract, you have to pay £1,000 pm for the next 21 months, a grand total of £21,000. Terrifying number when you look at it like that. But once you've accepted that is the case you can start to put the wheels in motion to create a solution. You've done the dog work as a coach for bugger all before, so in the worst case you can do it again. Or you now decide how many extra hours of coaching per month it's going to take in order to cover the fee without it affecting your income and just grind it out! Even do more and save the extra to get it paid off early. Are you starting to see some of the learnings here already? Business management, problem solving, money management, savings, long term commitment. It sounds crazy but these kinds of situations can really help make you a businessman or woman. In this example by the time the debt was cleared, which was actually cleared upfront in around 9 months I believe, this coach had expanded his business online, created a secondary arm to the company and was also selling kit.

To this day he still thanks that massive fuck up for his success because had it never happened he'd never have thought or had the need to diversify his business. And even more so, never would've realised that he never actually wanted his own gym in the first place! Because had that really been the dream, he would've just stuck in there and got loans or credit cards to keep the lights on and just ground until it became a success like many others in the same field and situation have done. Big lesson learnt the hard way ey.

We've spoken about my situation a few times through this book and I've Shared a few of my screw ups and learnings that led me to where I am now, all of which i'm extremely grateful for. But do you know what I think of when I say the word reincarnation in relation to business? For me it's not about simply just learning from your mistakes and hoping not to allow history to repeat itself. It's about waking up one day and excepting that you are human, you have floors and you will fuck up multiple times in multiple areas of your life. But you get to a point where when something happens you smile, say thanks and think about your next step almost in the same breath.

I think my reincarnation process started to happen once i found my direction and passion with both my career and social circles, and I truly believe that i wouldn't be in the position I feel I am now if it hadn't been for a lot of those lessons along the way. So do not be afraid to fail, be afraid to fail and come away from it having learnt absolutely nothing from the situation.

Just think, this book was born out of a global pandemic with no prior thought or belief to write a book. After tragedy struck, I thank the world for the opportunity to learn and grow and thought to myself, what next?

This book was only one of a handful of unbelievable things to have come from a real shit situation.

## Who Am I?

When I titled this chapter every ember in my body was telling me to place it at the start of the book to prompt a big meaningful thought straight off the bat, but there's a very specific reason it's here and obviously I'm going to tell you.

I believe that there is a tiny bit of truth in the words 'wisdom comes with age' man it pisses me off admitting that my parents were right ha. But it's true in life just as in business. As a PT it takes years (as you've already read at least 3) to even get a real grip on your shit and have a rhythm and still, I'm sure there are people out there who will disagree but most of which that I know also had a job waiting for them or were X professional sports people so floods of clients were just there from day dot. Major respect don't get me wrong but I come from the graft and I still feel I have to graft hard nowadays to stay at the top of my game.

The question of who am I comes up every year during a self evaluation period. Me and my wife actually have this for our relationship as well believe it or not. On every anniversary we go for a meal and talk it all out, how was the year?

The good, bad and fucking annoying! If there's anything that really would be an issue for each other long term we address it, finish with a shot and leave it all at the table. We have always left holding hands, so happy days. I do much the same with my business side of things;

Am I still enjoying it?

Have I achieved what I wanted to?

Am I on the right path?

And who am I within my space?

At this point in the book if you are a coach and have done the groundwork you should be able to answer at least 1 or 2 of the above questions with absolute certainty from your heart, this can be a lot harder than people think.

It's pretty scary when I realise how many people just do what they do in a robotic manner without ever even asking or acknowledging how they actually feel about it. To keep with the gym theme, life is much like a treadmill for many people, once they get on and start moving the sole focus seems to be just to stay on for as long as they can possibly hold on, but with zero plan of how to do that. If you're not able to answer the above about your job, regardless of what role you are in, I strongly suggest just stopping and taking a moment to breathe and think about it. Much like a treadmill interval I guess. Kick the feet up on the side plates and breathe.

*Who Am I?*

To know who you are and understand yourself in any industry you need to have been around long enough to have fucked up, learnt then fucked up over and over again in order to find a rhythm. It's only at this point, which I call the sweet spot, where our identity starts to shape. The surface level stuff is in place. We greet and manage people in a certain way, we have our systems in place to get the best results and we also know and understand (or at least start to) our worth. This is what I like to call the subconscious monotony or rhythm of our work. It's once we're not having to really concentrate on every single aspect of our day, we just simply do it, then we can start to reserve a little more time to figure our shit out.

I remember not too long ago once our whole business went online and we stopped PT. One thing no one considered was the effect on our own identity this was going to have. And I don't mean just sharing the so-called limelight with someone else, that really never has bothered me. What did  affect me was the feeling of not really being in control. I'd spent years building up not only my business but also my name as a coach and I was in control of absolutely every element, and every success or progression that came off the back of it had a route I understood. Pain in the ass at times but that's just how it is! Now  we had agents and a team to look after everything apart from the decision making process as to who we would work with and the general creative, that was still 100% on us. They do contracts, legal, finance and any conversation between an idea and you creating it. This saves time and energy for us to focus on the stuff we need to do and I'm still grateful for my team but one thing I totally fucked up on was letting them essentially do everything. This nearly cost us everything and I really mean that.

Not a lot of people know this but a couple years ago the TLM brand nearly went completely up the swanny. How? When I look back now, it's still easy to blame others but it was me and us who dropped the ball and if I had a true grip and understanding of who i really was at the time it would never have happened.

So in the online and social media industry when you get offered a job, you agree terms and creative etc then you sign contracts and create, awesome. Then you invoice and get paid within 3 months...... ish! You see with any single contract there could be 4 levels of communication between you and the physical spokesperson for the brand so things can take time, funnily enough more so when it comes to paying up it seems. At this point we had completely stopped PT and was not yet online coaching so everything was dependent on the online social pot staying full.We had a great year where we worked with some awesome brands, created some sick content and had a good laugh along the way. Even treated ourselves to a snowboarding holiday as we could easily afford it and wanted to just hang as buddies for once! At the end of the year our accountant text us and was like 'boys do you have any work lined up as we've nothing come in the account for over a year and we have about 10k left.......WTF! This was enough to cover our wages and outgoings for a further month, 2 max. We spoke to our team and

was obviously a bit frustrated as all our contracts say payment within 3 months but one invoice was over 15 months overdue! No one seemed to understand how this had happened but basically we were up the creek and owed a lot of money. After every one chased everything back and invoices with a stern legal note attached were sent out to piss takers, we had a meeting with the DM at our agency, possibly the lowest point in my adult career, this fucking sucked in fact!

For as long as I could remember I had been earning my own wage. We went in and had to ask for a 20k loan to cover ourselves until the money we were owed came back in and they would take it back as it did. They saw it as a shared fuck up so were happy to help. Which not many agents would do, it's reasons like this we are still with them today. But I came out with a taste in my mouth that was also a huge wake up call. For around a week I was like how the actual fuck did this happen and more importantly what do I do to ensure it NEVER happens again?! I'd stopped being in control of my shit and just 'rode the wave' this phrase pisses me off to this day, but it's the only way I can describe that couple of crazy years. I lost who I was, I became soft and and took the easy route.

I'm the type of person who creates and keeps my own rhythm by being in control of my own day and setting tasks to complete. It's pretty simple but I've said many times - I'm not built for employment. It simply doesn't test me enough, i'm by no means saying employed people are lazy, far from it. But if I have an idea and want to just make it happen I don't want to have to speak to a line of 6 managers to get a green light. For that couple of years I basically became employed by my own business instead of running it, an integral part of who I am today had been lost. I won't go into the detail on how our business changed  at this stage but essentially we spent all of our time up until this current day creating more than one revenue stream, so we were never dependent on a third party again. I'm thankful to say we hit that target and things are going well, mainly because i now understand who I am and own my own shit.

So when someone asks who you are, like truly, really take your time before answering. You may not even know yet, as it can take years to truly understand who you are and what your rhythm is. But once you know, hold on to that identity and lead your business with it because if you don't, well it could cost you literally everything you've worked for.

This is also why I dislike major long term goal setting, especially in the early days. Because these goals could be set and by the time you actually achieve them, you are a totally different person all together and could be left feeling deflated.

Ever felt like that chasing a physique or number on the scales? You get there then... ow ok mmm
Think on.

# Online Transition

I can guarantee at least ½ of you reading this who are already PT's just skipped straight to this chapter didn't ya? Haha. I don't blame you at all, it's a great way to go, especially if you would like to be a little less tied down by a singular environment.

Now I want to talk to you all about the transition into online, how I went about it and what I think you really need to consider prior to heading down that road. You have probably realised by now that I'm a 'full picture kind of guy'. I like to consider a decision from every angle before making the big ones (most of the time anyway).

First of all, every single coach with half a brain cell is going to tell you to get a ton of experience on the gym floor first, why? Because that's where you start to understand people. It sounds silly but you would be totally naive to presume that coaching is purely about visual observations and progressive overload, far from it. In order to be truly great at what you do (and that's what I want from anyone reading this to become) you have to understand people beyond a surface level. How they move, why they move that way and how to get them moving more effectively, whilst understanding boundaries both personally and professionally.

Then who are they, what makes them tick physically and emotionally, and most of all what they 'really' want from your help, because trust me it will never be just the 3 or 4 simple goals written down on the par-q. So in short, earn your stripes as they say, this will make it a lot easier for you online as you will have confidence and past clients to refer to in order to help market your services.

I need to clear one thing up before going any further as I feel a lot of successful coaches do not make this clear. Yes I have a successful online coaching business and have done all the graft to get here over years and years of hard work, but still a lot of people see this end product and presume it comes easy. If you are coaching and have maybe 20 clients face to face you should naturally presume that maybe 10-20% of those will transition to online with you, if you were expecting anymore than that you are potentially setting yourself up for disappointment.

Looking at your social reach, how many followers across how many outlets do you have? I see new PT's starting up a business page and going straight hard for online with 100 followers and zero reputation or raport wondering why it's just not working! For context we have over 100,000 followers on instagram right, and that on a standard day (if I mention online coaching) leads to 1 maybe 2 enquiries, which tends to lead to 1 or 2 clients who want to sign up weekly. That's a pretty decent conversion rate but when people see 100,000 or even just 100 followers on insta, they presume that's 100 clients, it really isn't. 80% of your audience will never want to purchase anything from you and the 20% that do won't all be ready at the same time or when you want them to be, so at this point I'm simply just trying to  help you to manage your expectations a little. If you've done everything right up until this point then you are most likely on to a winner and will find the next step quite easy, because you have now started separating your audience from the want to buy' and 'want to watch' groups.

Before you even choose your service provider and start planning your advertising campaigns you need to figure out what your product/products are and cement them first. Seems simple but online coaching isn't just PT'.

Clients want and need totally different things to the norm. You wanna know why PT in the gym is pretty simple, it's a singular product, you do it all or nothing, it's a ballsy but good way to start thinking about the online process. One thing JC and I decided from the off is that we would have a couple options in order to appeal to both sides of our audience, the educated and uneducated. That sounds harsh but a good 40% of clients we've had have actually been PT's themselves and they don't need as much as the general population.

So we offer one simple plan 95% of the year, the SILVER. It's very clear what you get and how it works. Very simple and I believe this is the way it needs to be for you as well. You don't need to overcompensate with some huge brochure and sales pitch just because you can't be there to talk people across the line. A lot of people still totally over complicate their products to the point where the consumer has no idea whether they're purchasing a PT product or qualifying for the Marine core, honestly i've read a few and i'm even reading the dictionary trying to figure out some of the useless fucking jargon in there, so don't do that.

Two times per year (and by no means do you have to do this) we run a 12 week challenge called 'surprise surprise' The GOLD Challenge. We hand pick 10 applicants who pay a little more than the usual for two reasons. One they get more of our time throughout the challenge and weekly calls. Two, one person walks away at the end with a free holiday, home gym or years gym membership paid for by us. It's a great and popular product but let me be clear and honest when I say this. It's not for everyone and no matter how many people want coaching or a free holiday, not all of them want to pay.

The product has risk on two parts. It has to be more expensive for obvious time reasons plus the fact that you have to spend a lot on the prize so recovering a least a little of that fee is helpful. Two there is zero idea of how many people are going to join up until the day. So the first time we ran the GOLD challenge we had 2 applicants join and both of which quit before the end for personal reasons, and honestly thank god as had we got to the end and picked a winner we would've ended at least £1,000 in the bin as the winners prize costs around £2,000 and of which 4 people have to run the whole course to even cover that let alone taking our daily wage as such in to the equation. These products are never about profit, they are always about brand awareness and giving back which has great value in itself.

Think of it like this, when deciding on the product, give enough information in order for the consumer to know pretty much exactly what they're getting and for how much, but basic enough that they may come back with a couple simple questions, that's where your work begins! Ow and YES put the fucking price on the product straight away, there's nothing more annoying for people then clicking through for more details and getting everything other than what they really wanted to know. And yes other coaches may well enquire just to get your prices as well but screw them, take it as a compliment!

So you have your product/s ready BOOM, what makes it different, what's your USP?! If you can not answer this question even on a simple level then don't go live with it! There's a 1,000 other PT's out there doing the same as you, why should I choose you as my coach? It's strong enough to say something like 'it's me who will program every single workout' or 'the level of support' .

Is there also a client specific phone number for them to use to contact you directly or are you just the best at what you do in your field? Answer these questions for yourself to get your product fully finished and shiny.

Product sorted? CHECK! Fab, now the part I actually really struggled with… this ain't no poxy excel spreadsheet world anymore ok! I know everyone appreciates a little bit of old school charm but you can't run an online coaching business via excel unless you either have all the hours under the sun or are simply going to be just changing the name
at the top of the plan and sending blanket plans to people…they look shit so don't do it. Sorry but it's true.

I use TrueCoach, it's simple for both me and the user and has everything I need, I also hear MyPTHub and Fitr are great but i've never used them for singular PT so i'll stick in my lane. Within a month of using TC I had this moment where i wished it had been around ten years ago. You have an individual profile for every single client, can
track practically every metric you can imagine and an exercise video catalogue which is vast to say the least. Literally cut my personal period-ised programming time down by ¾ straight away! And time is key right! Most importantly of all, every client i've had so far has gotten along with the interface well. There are plenty of people out there who will say "why don't you have your own and just use that? TrueCoach costs about £50pm and does everything I need. To build such a thing for myself would be around 5-10k and for what? It won't bring anymore clients in, so I say choose your financial battles here. Maybe one day it will be a must but right now it ain't broke so i'm not in a hurry to fix it! And before anyone starts panicking about having to pay monthly for such a service, trust me it's worth it and pays for itself very quickly.

Think of it like gym rent, the first week of coaching is there to cover the rent, 3 weeks is profit. Plus with TC the first 5 clients are free so by the time you have to pay you're already earning far more than you need to shell out for the app.

Next up the most important part, practice! Become a client and be on the end of your own programming. It still shocks me to this day when i speak to a coach who's using an online programming service but actually has no idea how it looks and works as a client! When I first downloaded the app I was the first client I ever signed up, I went through the profile building process, completed my own tailored test week and programmed myself for a full 2 week block of training ticking off every session as a client would. Why? Because if that interface is not yours directly you best know how to deal with any potential issues your clients might face with it. I even went to the point whereby I was sending comments and messages on the chat to see how long they took to come through. This led me to getting my second phone and I'm thankful for it in many ways not just because of this. I realised that anytime someone messaged or commented on their session it could take up to 2 hours to come through, not a problem… unless they're mid session and have no clue what an inverted row is and there's no video!

So I say to every client to communicate mainly through the phone and only comment on the workout if it doesn't require an answer right there and then.

Invaluable information to have right off the bat rather than having to scramble round finding a new phone at some point in the first month.

Only once all these stages have been ticked off are you ready to launch online, in my opinion this sets you up to have minimal stress down the road so i'd say it's worth the delay.

Now the easy parts out of the way let's get on with the real hard work, selling the damn thing!

First of all you are going to have to come to terms with the fact that the amount of 'free time' you give away is about to triple! When you walk round a gym with or without a client you are advertising yourself. But online, if you ain't posting no one is seeing you! I would say at a guess (rough guess) I put in around 20 hours of 'free time' for every client that comes on, in the form of instagram posts, stories, emails and youtube content. Some may say 'fuck that' but honestly it's a hustle and i'm not going to sit here and say any different. You have to create content around your niche and products, you have to also be very consistent, you can not just sling one advert out and think you'll never need to advertise again. Wanna know a little secret, I spend double the amount of time advertising our products when we are full as I do when we have spaces. A lot of people think that's stupid and a waste of time but I say this- I'd rather have a waitlist of people eager to get coaching, maybe even a little pissed off because they have to wait, than lose 60% of my clients at once when they're done and have to scramble to find new people. This can result in you having to work with maybe less favourable clients as well, because the focus goes away from your niche and more towards your bank account.

So I believe these to be the vital steps to get you off the ground, I hope they really help you feel more confident in the transition.

*It's a solitary ol thing*

Online coaching is by nature a very solitary job, some may say that's obvious but i wouldn't include this statement if it weren't important. PT face to face is possibly the most sociable job going, to the point where it can be physically exhausting just talking all day. To go from that to potentially only speaking to someone on a Friday via text as you do your weekly check ins can be a bit of a shock. I have a handful of clients right now who would 100% never message me if I didn't them. They have their program, know what to do and just tick it off. If you go from being in the gym 50 hours a week with people to having 30 online clients who are practically mute it may feel a bit shit. So it begs the question of whether you decide to go full send online or have an element of both.

My situation meant it had to be fully online but I do now see a face to face client occasionally , say once per month. Not necessarily for the social aspect but more to keep my hands on skills tuned, and I look forward to it every time.

If it's a route that you may want to go down i'd suggest having an exact cap for each face to face and online client then manage it well. This way you can decide exactly what days you will be in the gym and maybe discuss a slight discount from the gym rent as you won't be there all the time, then also reserve enough time for the online program management. Trust me there is a lot more work to be done online than you might first think.

For most PT's out there the job starts and finishes with the session, let's cut the shit that's how most people see it. That's one hour maybe more per week of practical execution. When you start programming someone, even if you are doing a simple 6 week block, 5 days per week and the exercises do not change in that time, that's still going to take a good few hours to write and get ready. Then every session that client completes you go in, check their feedback and videos if they add them and respond practically every day. X that by 30 and you are going to have a lot on your plate so make sure you schedule your time well!

## The Real Methods To Succeed

We've now arrived at that point in the book where I start tying things up in a little bow and sending you off into the brave world of coaching. So here's a couple extra tools I think you will benefit from.

If I sat here at 33 years of age and tried to tell you that I possess all of the answers, I hope you'd call the biggest bull shit on me right away because I believe you never stop learning, nor should you. In fact i'd go as far as to say, it's the first method to succeed in this space. As a PT it's very easy to believe you can only do it on your own or 'it's you against the world' but the second you believe that to be the truth, it will turn into your downfall. Establish your niche and be extremely passionate about it for sure, but do not become arrogant or closed off to others around you as they will help you grow.

With that in mind, a real comfort (not embarrassment that some feel) comes with opening yourself up to others. As PT's we are sometimes expected to have all the answers our clients could possibly ever need. Once we realise we don't and in some cases never will it makes it a lot clearer and easier to focus on what we should be doing.

I don't have a list of qualifications that I believe you should get under your belt either. This may also come as a surprise to many, but it's not about qualifications, well not solely anyway. First of all you can't do it all, that's what referrals are for. If a nutrition client comes in and you don't have the level of knowledge to help them are you gonna say 'wait 3 years mate, just gonna pop off and do a degree then i'll be with you!' No, well i hope not anyway otherwise you'll end up with a shit ton of knowledge and degrees hanging on the wall but no clients.

And if i've learnt nothing else as a coach i've learnt this - Your clients do not give a flying fuck about your understanding of the kreb cycle or what glycogen does and how it behaves in your body, and if you base your whole product around that then you will end up spending most of
your time dick swinging with other professionals rather than helping the people who really need your knowledge and care, the general
population. When my clients leave me I often ask them for a short write up on their experience, do you know what practically every single person mentions? That I offered support and showed care throughout their time.

You see, to me (and i'm not saying you have to be the same) coaching is about people and more importantly people's emotions and mental health. I genuinely couldn't care less if I had 500 people lose 2 stone each (which is quite an easy thing to achieve in fact) but if I had 500 people in my whole career who came to me with a poor level of self worth and appreciation for their body, but left feeling at least capable and confident, i'd be a very happy man.

I feel our industry far to easily get's lost and focussed on pure vanity and aesthetics that many coaches can very easily forget that we are working with people not robots. So if you really want to have a profound effect on someone, work with them' not just their goals. If you think that's just a way of saying i don't get results, then you've got me wrong!

There's one thing i'm always saying to my clients and that is 'you have to allow time for change to take place' or 'it doesn't happen overnight'.These two phrases are both loved and hated by me equally. Mainly hated because I feel i'm constantly saying it to clients lol But also loved because it's a constant reminder to myself as a coach.

In order to even be considered a 'good' coach it takes a lot of graft and time, it doesn't happen overnight!

I remember starting out and forever feeling like i wasn't doing well enough, didn't get enough results or didn't have enough clients, still do to this day at times. But I never stopped to ask myself if I was actually happy doing it! At every level of success, ask yourself 'am i happy?' I meet many people who train 2 clients per week, teach a couple classes and spring out of bed every day for their 15k per year salary, buzzing. So remember it's not all about total numbers, how you feel about them is what's most important.

*Fail Hard, Fail Well.* I've learnt the hard way so many times in my career and I'm sitting here waiting for the next lesson, trust me, they never stop coming. But failure is a huge part of the process and if you learn to fail well yourself, it will also make you a far better coach as you'll have experience in what to do when your clients do the same thing during their journey.

You see, failure whatever happens is not the important part at all, it's what you choose to do immediately next that really matters. Lay down and cry about it and feel sorry for yourself and basically learn nothing and leave yourself in a position to repeat the same failure again? Or break it down, assess the situation and learn from it.

A key phrase I live by nowadays is 'Don't Fail Twice!' I have this written on my whiteboard in the office and I see it every damn day. The phrase in itself tells you and should reassure you also that failures happen no matter what, but don't allow that behaviour to repeat itself again! I don't mean as in 'ever' I live by it as a simple rule week by week, day by day.

If I miss a training session on Monday for whatever reason 'don't fail twice' pops into my head and guess what i'm not missing Tuesday.. Yep my fucking training session! I even go as far as saying it becomes a higher priority the very next day through missing it as well.

Try it!

## The Future

Now that word, 'future' it can be your best friend or worst enemy depending on how you choose to use it. Having got to this point in the book you will notice that practically everything I have spoken about is in relation to getting yourself going and getting to the next level and understanding who you are as a coach right. Something that has to be considered throughout your career is the future, what next and more importantly how?

As I have said there is no need' to forward plan if your goal is to coast and do ok' but for the rest of you there's a few things that are really going to help.

*Set Annual Goals* - They do not all have to be about financials either! It's a common misconception with goal setting that it's all about money, probably half the reason it puts people off in the first place. But as a species we need to aim for something, we need to have a purpose as such. I do it like this;

GOAL 1 - Business Related *(financial growth, educational growth, numbers and targets, new product etc)*

GOAL 2 - Personal Goal *(self development, training, material purchase, gifting)*

GOAL 3 - Family Goal *(give more time, presence, family trips)*

GOAL 4 - My Bonus - this is the final goal and it's pretty self explanatory. Once i've set my other goals I decide what i'm going to reward myself with when i complete them all. This year it was a new top spec MacBook 'which i'm writing this book on' soooo I completed my goals.

The fourth is optional but I do believe that good behaviours should be rewarded in life and who rewards you when you're self employed if not?

I will take the Business Goal to use as an example, but every goal should be broken down and set up the same.

Say i wanted the business to grow by £10,000 over the next year. Great what next?
So £10,000 divided by 12 = £833. We need to grow financially month on month by £833.
With an average of 30 days in a month, divide £833 by 30 = £27.76p per day.

So in order for me to grow my business by 10k I need to be making £27.76p per day. Still a challenge but that number actually starts to look a lot more in my ballpark, a goal I can hit, a goal that gets me hungry instead of intimidated. Once you have your daily and weekly target, pin that fucker up on the wall or on your whiteboard so you don't forget it.

Next you look at all of your products and their current income. As a PT nine times out of ten, the only product you have is yourself, so if your target is to gross an extra £27.76 per day.

You first look for the obvious space whereby you could add extra clients or teach more classes. Say once you've plugged the gaps it ends up bringing you a solid extra income of £20 on average per day spread across the month, brilliant but unless you duplicate yourself you're still short by £7.76pd. What's another product you can offer or make? Most coaches come up with a slogan or brand name they can sell as merch and get their clients to wear and take a solid 60/70% commission on sales. Sweet earner.

You get the point here. What I like to do with my annual goals is break them down into monthly targets which in turn get broken down into weekly targets. Yep you guessed it, they then become my daily targets…. Which go up on my whiteboard. Tah dah you have your daily to do lists sorted already.

I also set monthly and quarterly alerts in my diary to check in on progress of all goals in case somethings falling behind and needs more attention, or somethings flying and I need not put more energy in unless I reassess the goal.

The good thing with setting goals longer term to begin with is, it forces you to grow mentally before you do physically. Even in that example above the goal was to grow the financial side of the business and the second thing I thought to do was create a brand new product. This may have never entered my mind if i'd not looked to the future and forced myself to think outside the box. Trust me many incredible creators and business people alike start with the idea, goal or problem, then track back to find the route to solving it.

*The Future*

This may sound a little harsh to some but my ultimate goal each year is, honestly to look back at myself from the exact same time the year before and almost be embarrassed by the person I was. Growth is a really important thing to me, in every area I want to grow year on year. Be a better dad, husband, athlete, businessman the lot.

Another tip when thinking about that word, the 'future' is to decide '*what next*' I'm not saying by any means that you can't be on the gym floor doing a PT session with old Dot and Terry in your 60's, rock on if that's your dream chase it! But in reality the majority of PT's I meet love it in their 20/30's then they hit this point where they either stop appealing to the younger clients so the numbers fall or lifestyle changes and forces them to change with it, it happens!

By having a plan as to what you want to do next, it won't only help you to build your goals year on year, it will also give you an end game that many don't think about. Do you want to run your own gym, do you want to become an educator, do you want to train PT's or clients?

You may be thinking 'hang on Leon's in his mid 30's and he's writing a book for PT's' haha Don't jump to fast people. My goal is still very much to coach clients, the enthusiasm and love I still have for that is beyond huge, whether that be 121 clients or just watching members of the TLM Training Plans kick arse, I love it all. But I have made a conscious move over the last year to help people in the industry more. I've had over ten great years in it and I'm still going strong, so I have a lot to thank the fitness world for. I want to help other coaches realise their true potential and follow their dreams and offer them a helping hand along the way, this book is the first step.

*Out sourcing* - We touched upon outsourcing very briefly when talking about potentially bringing in another PT etc and scoring a commission. But down the line, especially if the goal is to transition and scale your business online, is outsourcing.

This by far is the hardest thing for me and JC to do with our business! As a coach you are the identity of your own company, you're the reason people come for coaching and you are the person they expect to see at the door right.
There are many areas of your business that are not front facing that you can outsource when the time is right. Try not to think of it as money going out of your pocket, think of it as freeing up more time for you to grow. Hiring an accountant to do everything from payroll, invoices and VAT etc has not only saved a ton of time month on month but a lot A LOT of stress as well. I remember when we first brought him in, all I could think about was the cost! By the time the next VAT bill came round he'd given me back so much of my wasted time the business had grown.

Some people outsource for all emails, DM's, enquiries the lot and from what i hear it's not that expensive. It doesn't mean you are lazy, nor does it mean you couldn't do it yourself, it just means you would rather spend your time on the key important roles you have. So think about that as you start to scale the business. It also helps drive a little distance between you and your potential audience/clients making it harder for them to get 'you' the golden egg which helps increase value as well.

But like I say, we're terrible at that. I still reply to every email and enquiry that comes in, we both write our own programs and coach every 121 client ourselves, and do our DM's haha but whatever floats your boat.

## Summary And References

It's time for me to go..

If i haven't bored you to death by now I would like to say thank you. Thank you for taking the time to read through this book cover to cover. As I said this was a personal project of mine so it really didn't matter if not a single person got to this point. I'd already completed my objective, but I will say it means the bloody world to know you have. So a little test for ya, if you get to this point in the book do me a favour and DM me on Instagram @Leonbusty or @theleanmachinesofficial saying 'Yes Leon I finished it okk!'

I would love to sit here and say this book is my life's work and I have shared all my knowledge and understanding of the world and industry I work in, but that would be a lie. The goal with this book was to share a tool kit for PT's out there to really make it and find their feet in the industry, along with a large biography of my experience and life up to now. I believe as a coach the thing our industry lacks is support and education in the real practical world. It's all good and well getting all the certificates you need but in the real world we need real people, real advice and a basic understanding of business, I don't know about you but man I lacked that and I really wish I had someone to teach me. So if you've learnt a single thing in that respect i'm truly happy for you!

Also I want to take this moment to say a huge thank you to a great friend of mine Chelsea for proof reading this so you lot could make some sense of it all. Go check her out on Instagram - @chelsealeanutrition

All of what I have written is my own opinions and learnings but there are a few people out there right now doing incredible things in different areas, along with some great book recommendations that I think you will really benefit from reading or listening to in many areas not just PT or training.

Books
Ego Is The Enemy
*Ryan Holiday*
The Obstacle Is The Way
*Ryan Holiday*
Atomic Habits
*James Clear*
Essentialism
*Greg McKeown*
Tribe Of Mentors
*Tim Ferriss*

Can't Hurt Me
*David Goggins*
*Paul Mort Will Save Your Life*
Paul Mort
L

Printed in Great Britain
by Amazon